MACKINTOSH
ARCHITECTURE

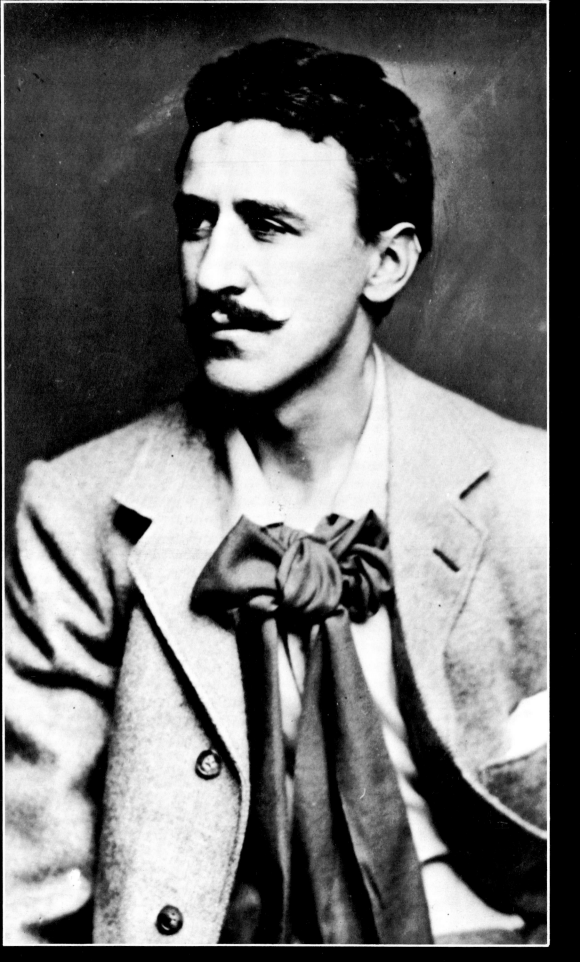

MACKINTOSH
ARCHITECTURE

The Complete Buildings and Selected Projects

Edited by Jackie Cooper   Foreword by David Dunster   Introduction by Barbara Bernard

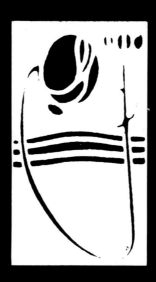

ACADEMY EDITIONS · LONDON/ST. MARTIN'S PRESS · NEW YORK

ACKNOWLEDGEMENTS
We would like to thank the following individuals
and institutions for the loan of and for permission
to reproduce photographs and drawings: T. and
R. Annan and Sons Ltd., Glasgow; Mr. and Mrs.
H. Jefferson Barnes; Mr. Tim Benton; The Glasgow School of Art; Messrs. Keppie, Henderson
and Partners; Mr. P.E.P. Norton; The Royal
Commission on the Ancient and Historical Monu-
ments of Scotland, for photographs by Bedford
Lemere; The Scottish Arts Council; Hunterian Art
Gallery, University of Glasgow, Mackintosh Col-
lection.
   Special thanks also to Roger Billcliffe and Joan
Hughson (University of Glasgow, Fine Arts De-
partment) for verifying information and for advice,
and to the Charles Rennie Mackintosh Society for
their help.
   The map of Mackintosh buildings in the City of
Glasgow is reproduced courtesy of Strathclyde
Regional council, (Glasgow Sub-Region), Roads
Department.
   In addition we would like to express our
gratitude to Mr. H. Jefferson Barnes of the
Glasgow School of Art and Mr. Robert Rogerson
of the Royal Incorporation of Architects in Scotland Hill House Trust for permission to photograph these buildings, and to Andre Goulancourt
for his colour photographs.

Captions to colour plates:

I-V GLASGOW SCHOOL OF ART
I   North elevation, detail of main entrance from
       Renfrew Street.
II   Library, view from the North-West.
III   The Second of the two boardrooms.
IV   Director's office, staircase leading to private
       studio.
V   Director's office showing a range of Mackin-
       tosh's furniture.

VI-X HILL HOUSE, HELENSBURGH
VI   View from the South, detail of garden eleva-
       tion.
VII   View from the South-West.
VIII   Drawing room looking North.
IX   Master bedroom looking East.
X   Master bedroom looking West.

Frontispiece — Charles Rennie Mackintosh, 1903.
(Annan)

Published in the United States of
America by St. Martin's Press
175 Fifth Avenue
New York NY 10010

Library of Congress
Catalog Card Number 83-51780
ISBN 0-312-50244-3 (USA only)

Published in Great Britain by
Academy Editions
7 Holland Street
London W8

CONTENTS

Charles Rennie Mackintosh,
1920. Photograph by O. E.
Hoppé. (GSA)

FOREWORD

This volume contains the architectural projects of Charles Rennie Mackintosh organised in three parts: the executed buildings, alterations and interiors and finally some of his unexecuted designs and competition entries. By comparison with other 'Art Nouveau' architects like Guimard, Mackintosh's output never encompasses other stylistic traits. For as Barbara Bernard's introductory essay points out, he was above all an architect obsessed by the craft of building. Pevsner, for whom building and architecture are two entirely separate categories, recognises this and comments that in the hands of Mackintosh 'building becomes an abstract art, both musical and mathematical' (*Pioneers of Modern Design*, 1960, p. 169).

It is of course well known that Mackintosh seized the possibility of designing a total work of art — furniture, fittings, curtains, cutlery etc. And to some extent this amazing skill can blind the eye to the extraordinary ingenuity displayed in manipulating both space and its enclosing surfaces. For in many of the rooms the question of what is furniture what building is totally blurred, and the distinction becomes more and more un-interesting the more the work is examined. It becomes clear that for Mackintosh furniture and space were merely categories of design within which motifs of workmanship were precisely scaled to the material being used. The totality of both seems, however, to avoid that totally unusable geometricising which could make, for example, Frank Lloyd Wright's interiors a visual delight and a literal pain in the back. There is always a variety of scales between the whole room and that surface in immediate contact with the human hand. The organising principle is two-fold: firstly that geometry and the right angle pre-dominate, and secondly that whatever scale is used is related to function.

Mackintosh's debt to the aphorism that construction should be decorated and not decoration constructed is total. But beyond that he exploits geometrical orderings, whether of panel or grid, suggesting depth where little exists in his use of the former and allowing light to penetrate everywhere via the grids. The almost aetiolated natural forms, distended beyond the natural appearance of flowers or plants, suggests that he extended the aphorism into his decoration also. For there can be little doubt that the decorative forms are clearly a halfway house between nature and the possibilities of the material in which nature was to be represented.

Mackintosh never became a truly modern architect in the sense that his architectural obsessions could not be carried forth into new ways of planning, nor into industrially mass-produced elements. As with so many of his generation their lessons lie not so much in the organisation of their plans, which ultimately depend on some human hierarchy of haves and have nots, but in the spatial and constructional experiments which produced such a translucent and astonishing object as the Glasgow School of Art. In this building various scales are successfully united both inside and out, a difficult site is unequivocally brought into human use, and if it is easy to become obsessed with its components a visit will soon correct the photographic impression of a series of gems. This architect took Scotland, and England, into the twentieth century.

David Dunster
London, 1980

INTRODUCTION

Charles Rennie Mackintosh was born in Glasgow on 7 June, 1868, son of a police superintendent and one of a family of eleven. When Mackintosh was ten, the family moved from their tenement in the east end of Glasgow to a house in the suburbs, where the children were able to share their father's interest in tending what they called 'the Garden of Eden', a carefully cultivated patch of land attached to a nearby vacated residence. Mackintosh's uneventful childhood was further highlighted by regular lone rambles into the surrounding countryside, where he would observe and sketch flowers and buildings. These excursions, instigated by the family doctor in the interests of Charles' health, not only nurtured the boy's interest during his formative years in art and architecture — an interest which had no foundation in the family heritage — but also laid the foundation of an architectural vocabulary he was to use throughout his career. From an early age, Mackintosh had a desire to become an architect.

In 1884, at the age of 16, Mackintosh was apprenticed to the architectural office of John Hutchison. In the same year he enrolled for evening classes at the Glasgow School of Art. There were few possibilities at the time for architectural training beyond a narrow apprenticeship rooted in the stylistic wrangles of the preceding generation, where the aspiring young architect would struggle for responsibilities beyond the adornment of his master's structure. Mackintosh was fortunate. In 1889, when he was 21, he became a junior draughtsman in the busy offices of Honeyman and Keppie, a large, prosperous architectural practice in Glasgow, where commissions, such as the extension to the Glasgow Herald building and Queen Margaret's Medical College — considered minor projects not warranting the attentions of a senior member of the firm — were placed in the hands of juniors such as Mackintosh. As a result, Mackintosh's reputation as an original architect soon spread. The *British Architect* wrote in 1895 of the perspective drawing for the extension to the Glasgow Herald building: 'This admirable drawing sets forth one of the most noticeable modern buildings in Glasgow, a building which may fairly claim to be a genuinely modern development and — what so many clever things miss — not innocent of a quality of proportion and emphasis such as makes architecture a thing independent of mere style'. (*British Architect* xliii, 8 February 1895, p.94).

Moreover, the Glasgow School of Art had become a centre of artistic advance thanks to the influence of its head Francis Newbery, and his stress on creative individuality and progressive thinking. The emphasis placed by the school on the use of natural forms as artistic sources, the sensitive use of materials and techniques, and the harmonising of disparate artistic sources and references, laid the foundations of the modern style. Mackintosh subscribed whole-heartedly to these principles, and in conjunction with his like-minded colleague from Honeyman and Keppie and fellow student Herbert McNair, and later with the two Macdonald sisters at the School of Art (Herbert McNair was to marry Frances Macdonald in 1899, Mackintosh married Margaret in 1900), he formed 'The Four', a group dedicated to the search for a distinctive modern style, a search influenced by the opposing ideologies of Pre-Raphaelitism and Aestheticism. In 1896 The Four exhibited at the Arts and Crafts Society in London, where they showed highly stylised furniture, craftwork and graphics which, while unacceptable to the traditionalist majority, caught the attention of *The Studio*. This magazine exerted a strong influence on The Four through its publication of work by artists such as Beardsley, Toorop and Voysey, and was to greatly encourage them, Mackintosh in particular, through its regular appreciation of their work. The poetic, curvilinear style of The Four, which earned them the name of the 'Spook School', was a precursor of the Art Nouveau movement. But, while McNair and the Macdonald sisters continued to tend fervently in this direction, Mackintosh remained somewhat remote, maintaining a regard for the monumentality of Classicism and searching further for an aesthetic that would combine the linear sensitivity of the Spook School with the regard for solidity and structural logic characteristic of the thinking of Ruskin, Mackintosh's favourite author.

Mackintosh was from the outset a highly successful student, winning prizes in 1885 and 1886 from the School of Art, and in 1887 from the Glasgow Institute of Architects for the best set of building construction lecture notes and for measured drawings of the Royal Exchange, Glasgow. In 1888 he was awarded the prize for the best set of three-monthly designs and for his design 'A town house in a terrace', and in the same year the Bronze Medal at South Kensington for his 'Mountain Chapel' design. In 1889 he was awarded one of the National Queen's prizes at South Kensington for his design 'A Presbyterian Church', and in the same year he won a free studentship as well as the Glasgow Institute's design prize. In 1890 he was awarded the Alexander Thomson Travelling Scholarship for the best original design for a Public Hall in the Early Classical style, an award which enabled him in 1891 to undertake an extremely valuable tour of Italy, where he recorded his visits to famous Italian buildings in numerous sketches and diary entries. His reactions to what he saw are at times illuminating. He described the 'strange projections' and 'striking irregularities' of the Ducal Palace in Venice with unbounded enthusiasm, and the colours of sanctity in Florence Cathedral with a sensitivity to the function of the building undaunted by his admittedly 'profane' sentiments. On his return Mackintosh presented his drawings and gave a talk to the Glasgow School of Art, bringing him to the attention of its principal Francis Newbery, who became an important patron and influential friend. A comment in *Building News* in 1892 concerning the 'Italian Renaissance' character of Mackintosh's Chapter House design suggests that he was to some extent influenced by the buildings he saw in Italy. There is, however, no further evidence of an Italian stylistic influence subsequent to his Italian tour, although it undoubtedly resulted in an increased confidence and maturity of style.

Shortly after his return from Italy, Mackintosh delivered a paper entitled 'Scottish Baronial Architecture' to the Glasgow Architectural Association, a paper which, though to a large extent merely an admiring echo of the recently published volumes of MacGibbon and Ross's *Castellated and Domestic Architecture of Scotland*, neverthe-

The Glasgow School of Art, West door. (Annan)

less placed a very particular emphasis on the concept of an architecture native 'by absorption' and which proposed a development of the Scottish Baronial style beyond the sphere of domestic architecture.

The Scottish Baronial style represented to Mackintosh that monumentality which had distracted him from the 'icy perfections' of self-conscious stylistics. The austerity of the style appealed to his sensibilities, while its links with his Scottish heritage helped him to define a rational modernity in which indigenous references, natural to their human environment and in harmony with the surrounding landscape, could function beyond the restrictions of time.

In 1895 the governors of the Glasgow School of Art, having procured a site of 3,000 square yards and the sum of £21,000 from various sources, invited entries from eleven architectural firms, among them Honeyman and Keppie, for the design for a new building to accommodate the school and its ever increasing number of students. Competitors were asked to work within the limit of £14,000 to cover everything except the assessors' fees, painting, and the retaining wall, a sum deemed sufficient for nothing but a plain building. The governors subsequently altered their requirements, asking competitors to state what proportion of their design could be built for the specified £14,000, and to estimate the total cost of building. Francis Newbery indicated his requirements in terms of the number and dimensions of classrooms, and the sizes and nature of windows, which were to be sufficiently large to allow for good light in the studios.

In January 1897, three months after the submission of designs by competitors, the governors met to announce the winning entry — by Mackintosh, for Honeyman and Keppie. Mackintosh had designed an extremely plain building whose interest lay not in costly decoration or elaborate adornment, but in the measured asymmetry of its façades, and its unusual presentation of structural features. The scheme suited the taste and requirements of Francis Newbery, who did not share the general condemnation of the design as 'Art Nouveau'.

In 1897 building commenced on the Eastern section of the Glasgow School of Art, up to and including the entrance hall, which was completed in December 1899. Between 1906 and 1907 Mackintosh completely redesigned the West wing, incorporating the library, which was completed in 1909. It is interesting to follow the design alterations made by Mackintosh as building progressed, as an indication of his stylistic development, while the essential qualities which characterised Mackintosh's architecture in general can be seen in the completed School of Art, widely recognised as the first building in the modern style.

Mackintosh saw building not as a single creative act, but as a social process in which the adaptation of the original design to suit the changing needs of the client was vital. He altered the design of Hill House, for example, while building progressed, to accommodate a nursery for a new baby — an unexpected addition to the Blackie family. Alterations to the original design for the School of Art, however, were determined rather by Mackintosh's stylistic evolution during the decade between the inception and completion of the project. The abandonment of Classical details, such as pilasters and cornices on the North front, resulted from the increasing austerity of his style. The West front, originally very ordinary in design, became a daring exploitation of line and space, with 25 foot windows providing a vertical emphasis in contrast to their horizontal arrangement in irregular groupings, while the glass wall of the conservatory jutted out some 15 feet into space, 80 feet above ground level. In the library, probably the most important interior of the School in terms of design, Mackintosh adapted the curvilinear style to exist on a small scale, subtly integrated into the overall design which, by contrast, is characterised by the taut, bold horizontals and verticals of structural elements.

In about 1905 (the date is uncertain) Mackintosh delivered a paper to a literary society outlining his belief in the three fundamental principles of architecture as 'usefulness', 'strength' and 'beauty'. While Mackintosh's contribution to modern architecture must be seen essentially in terms of what he built, rather than as a theoretician, his interpretation of these three principles is important to an understanding of his work, and to the design of the School of Art in particular. In his discussion of strength, Mackintosh stressed the visual appearance of mass, through the use of materials, such as stone, characterised by sturdiness and bulk, a quality evident throughout Mackintosh's structural work and which complements the extreme delicacy with which he handled the decoration of domestic interiors. This particular interpretation of strength, seen in the context of the use by modern architects of strong but visually light materials such as plate glass and steel, places Mackintosh within a particular tradition of modernism.

Usefulness, implying the direct relationship between function and design, is exemplified above all by the large West windows of the School of Art which light the two storeys of the library, while in the case of domestic projects such as Hill House, Mackintosh respected the function of home as enclosure by allowing solid walls precedence over small windows. The extent to which Mackintosh adhered to the principle of usefulness can be seen in his designs for Miss Cranston's tea rooms and their furniture, in which he not only made allowances for the anticipated crowds by reducing the visual weight of features such as light fittings (which were suspended on wires) to a minimum, but designed chairs with high backs to accommodate the ladies of Glasgow with their high hairstyles and hats.

Beauty represented to Mackintosh an intricate combination of three qualities: 'truth' or the use of materials according to their nature and the honesty of a building's façade in relation to the arrangement of space on its interior; 'decorated construction' a principle derived from the functionalist argument of Pugin; and 'association' or 'tradition', in particular the use of indigenous stylistic elements. Mackintosh's use of materials conforms strictly to his ideal. There is no evidence of scoring in plaster, veneering in wood, or unnecessary refinements in any sense. In the School of Art he made particular reference to the need for economy by retaining the raw state of materials wherever possible, as in the bare brick of the pavilion corridor, exposed steel roof-ties and rivets, the use of rough-sawn timber and unfinished cement rendering, and exposed joints. In the case of woodwork and furniture Mackintosh, abhoring the use of varnish or graining, either painted wood enamel white or used stains, usually almost black or dark olive green, to reveal the grain of the wood. The 'truth' of the façade is faithfully acknowledged in the design for the School of Art especially in the West façade, in which not only does the elevation relate stylistically and expressively to the plan, but the misalignments and disparities that exist on the level of the façade are in direct functional relationship to the arrangement of space on the interior.

Mackintosh's firm belief that 'construction should be decorated, and not decoration constructed', in other words that 'the salient and most requisite features should be selected for ornamentation', he applied with great rhythm and inventiveness, especially

Below left — Mains Street, the drawing room. (From *The Studio,* 'Modern British Domestic Architecture and Decoration', Summer 1901, p.113)

Below — Leaded mirror in the Room de Luxe, Willow Tea Rooms.

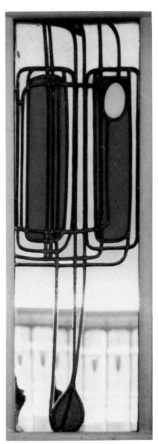

Hill House, view from the South-East. (Annan)

in those projects, such as the Glasgow School of Art and Scotland Street School, where budgets were severely limited. It has been suggested that Mackintosh's development of the modern style in these buildings can be largely attributed to the need, in both cases, for economy. The window brackets on the North front of the School of Art were not intended simply as decorative motifs, but for their vital function as rests for window cleaners' ladders. His decorative motifs, confined to doorways, windows, railings and so on, are always simple, reduced to their essence, often stylised abstractions of those natural forms which Mackintosh spent so long studying and drawing.

Perhaps his most uncompromising work in this respect was the unexecuted 1898 design for a concert hall, part of his entry for the 1901 Glasgow International Exhibition Buildings Competition. The circular structure was to be completely devoid of ornament, its bold effect being achieved by virtue of its proportion and structural elements — particularly its saucer-shaped dome and the twelve solid buttresses, rhythmically punctuated by long windows.

Mackintosh's insistence on 'association' or 'tradition' must be seen not as a wish to slavishly imitate or indiscriminately adopt the Scottish Baronial style, but rather to carefully absorb relevant elements of that style while adapting them to modern materials, methods and requirements. The dominance of solid over void, the use of stair turrets such as at Windyhill and Hill House (a feature of Scottish architecture between the 16th and 18th centuries), and in general the austerity characteristic of many of Mackintosh's buildings, are all references to the Scottish Baronial tradition which nevertheless do not detract from the essentially modern spirit of his style.

The Glasgow School of Art was constructed over a period of a decade, during which time Mackintosh became, in 1904, a partner in Honeyman and Keppie, and undertook several other projects, including Windyhill, Hill House, and various interiors and alterations. His interiors became, during these years, entirely confident in their expression of space and purpose. At Mains Street, the Mackintoshes first apartments after their marriage in 1900, Mackintosh created the first of his white rooms. Its sparse arrangement of specially designed furniture, and its restrained use of light colours — limited to white, pale grey for the carpet and canvas wall panels, and some square insets of coloured gesso — were commended by *The Studio* for its 'feeling of freshness, which is never monotonous'. Avoiding closed form and space through the use of open stairwells (as in the Willow Tea Rooms), decorative panels of repetitive vertical arrangement and unframed, and open-plan spaces in which the functional areas were separated from each other by screens (as at Hous'Hill), Mackintosh defined a new kind of space, unrestricted by static proportion. His ability to differentiate one room from

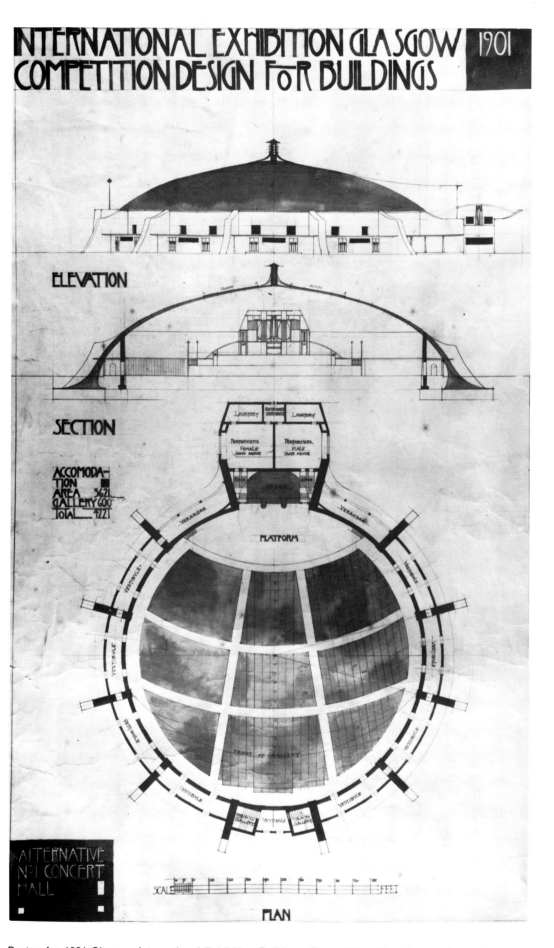

INTERNATIONAL EXHIBITION GLASGOW 1901
COMPETITION DESIGN FOR BUILDINGS

ELEVATION

SECTION

ACCOMODA-
TION
AREA 3621
GALLERY 600
TOTAL 4221

LAVATORY ENTRANCE VESTIBULE LAVATORY

PERFORMERS FEMALE SAME ABOVE   PERFORMERS MALE SAME ABOVE

ORGAN

VERANDAH   VERANDAH

PLATFORM

VESTIBULE   VESTIBULE

VESTIBULE   VESTIBULE

VESTIBULE   VESTIBULE

VESTIBULE   VESTIBULE

FRONT OF GALLERY

VESTIBULE   VESTIBULE

ALTERNATIVE
N°1 CONCERT
HALL

SCALE   FEET

PLAN

Design for 1901 Glasgow International Exhibition Buildings Competition. Elevation, section and plan of Alternative Concert Hall — detail. Pencil and wash on cream paper. (UGMC).

another through the use of distinctive light fittings, furniture, decoration and usage of space suited to the purpose and intended mood of each room is particularly evident in Miss Cranston's Tea Rooms, projects which offered Mackintosh great scope for whimsical variety, and in which he fully exercised that attention to detail which stemmed from his total involvement with each project. Mackintosh's interest in furniture, and the time and care he gave to its design, must be seen as integral to this involvement, while the effects of that interest are evident in the original way he handled the joints in beams, banisters, balusters, structural columns and so on.

Following the completion of the School of Art in 1909, Mackintosh's career began a steady decline, due in part to problems with clients over building costs — a problem consequent upon Mackintosh's desire for perfection in every detail. There were few commissions between 1909 and 1911, in which year he designed interiors for the Cloister Room and the Chinese Room at Miss Cranston's Ingram Street Tea Rooms. These projects indicate the continuing evolution of Mackintosh's style towards a strictly modern interpretation of line and form. In the Chinese Room especially, while preserving the whimsical tone implied in the room's name and function, Mackintosh entirely abandoned the curves of his early style and accentuated the severe rectilinear forms introduced into the final stages of the Glasgow School of Art building. The repetitive squares of the lattice screens and wall panels in the Chinese Room, and the geometrical line decoration of the Cloister Room, all testify to this development.

In 1913, under considerable strain from the pressures of office life and the demands of clients, Mackintosh resigned his position at Honeyman and Keppie. His capacity for rigorous work severely impaired by excessive drinking and damaged confidence, he and Margaret Macdonald left the 'philistine' city of Glasgow in 1914 for Suffolk, where Mackintosh intended taking up painting seriously. In 1915 the Mackintoshes moved once again, this time to Chelsea, at that time the artistic centre of London. His physical and mental health somewhat recovered, Mackintosh began once again to undertake various architectural projects, amongst them alterations to and interiors for a house in Northampton, a venture which proved successful and which further indicates that change in Mackintosh's style already apparent in the Ingram Street Tea Rooms towards tight, geometrical design, reminiscent of the Art Deco that was to come. Unfortunately, the outbreak of war hindered building and, while he produced designs for several other buildings, most of them in London, only one was carried out — the studio in Glebe Place for Harold Squire — and this in greatly diminished form. In 1928, at the age of 60, Mackintosh died after a brief illness, of cancer of the throat, in a Hampstead nursing home. Margaret Macdonald died in obscurity four years later.

After his early success, which was in itself tinged with misunderstanding and some contention, Mackintosh became gradually alienated from the architectural establishment, and while he was held in high regard by some — principally *The Studio*, the Austrian Secessionists, Francis Newbery, and the more sympathetic of his clients, the statement that he made in his structures and interiors passed for the most part unnoticed, unaccepted or mis-read. It was a statement whose syntax was divided between the functionalism of Pugin and the 19th century, the concern with craftsmanship in detail of the Arts and Crafts Movement, the language of the Scottish Baronial, and, to an increasing extent, the vision of the Modern Movement, which finally established itself about five years after Mackintosh's death. Half a century later, we have come to terms with the innovations and with the discrepancies that combine so sensitively in Mackintosh's style.

ABBREVIATIONS
Picture credits abbreviated in parentheses after captions are as follows:
Annan — T. and R. Annan and Sons Ltd.
Benton — Tim Benton.
GSA — The Glasgow School of Art.
Howarth — *Charles Rennie Mackintosh and the Modern Movement*, by Thomas
    Howarth, London, 1958.
Jefferson Barnes — Mr. & Mrs. H. Jefferson Barnes.
Norton — Mr. P. E. P. Norton.
RCAM — Royal Commission on Ancient Monuments, Scotland. *Crown Copyright*
UGMC — Hunterian Art Gallery, University of Glasgow, Mackintosh Collection.

COMMISSIONS
FOR
BUILDINGS

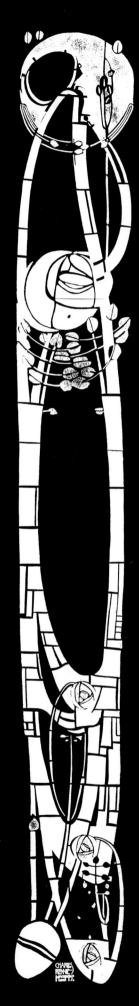

REDCLYFFE

Now 140 Balgrayhill Road, Springburn, Glasgow
Client: William Hamilton. Built 1890, extant. Now houses the Corporation Parks Department.

Mackintosh's first commission — a pair of semi-detached houses built for his uncle. Competently though unimpressively designed, these sturdy buildings are in red sandstone, with slate roofs.

No known drawings exist.

GLASGOW HERALD BUILDING MITCHELL STREET EXTENSION

Corner Mitchell Street and Mitchell Lane, Glasgow
Client: 'Glasgow Herald' newspaper. Built 1895, extant.

The newspaper offices were designed in 1893-94 by the firm of Honeyman & Keppie, where Mackintosh was a junior draughtsman. How much of the design can be directly attributed to Mackintosh is difficult to assess, but in the unusual handling of the water tower his influence is particularly felt. The stone building harmonises with the High Street 'Scottish Baronial,' built in 1891.

A perspective by Mackintosh was published in *Academy Architecture,* VI, 1894, p.89, in *The British Architect,* XLIII, 8 February 1895, p.98, with a description on p.94, and the building was also illustrated in Hermann Muthesius' *Die Englishe Baukunst der Gegenwart,* Berlin, 1900. Mackintosh undoubtedly executed the presentation perspective drawing of 1893-94, the earliest surviving of his professional drawings from his association with Honeyman & Keppie. The perspective is held in the University of Glasgow Mackintosh Collection.

FACING PAGE
Design for the Mitchell Street extension, Glasgow Herald Building. Perspective drawing, 1893-1894. Pen and ink 91.2 × 60.8 cm. (UGMC)

Below — Redclyffe, view from the West. (Annan)

THE "HERALD" BUILD.
MITCHELL St GLAS
OW. JOHN HONEYMAN AND KEPPIE

QUEEN MARGARET'S MEDICAL COLLEGE

Hamilton Drive, Glasgow

Client: University of Glasgow. Built 1894, extant – but extensive interior modifications and major structural alterations have been made to accommodate the needs of BBC Studios.

This women's medical college, thought to be the first such institution in Britain, was officially a Honeyman & Keppie commission and while ostensibly designed by John Keppie, Mackintosh's hand can be strongly detected thoughout this small, plain, red sandstone building.

His perspective drawing of 1894 was published in the *British Architect,* XLV, 10 January 1896, p.22. The drawing belongs to Keppie, Henderson & Partners, Architects, successors to Mackintosh's old firm, Honeyman & Keppie.

Design for Queen Margaret's Medical College. Perspective drawing, 1894. Pen and ink 49.8 × 80.6 cm. (Messrs. Keppie, Henderson and Partners)

MARTYR'S PUBLIC SCHOOL

Parson Street, Glasgow
Client: School Board of Martyr's Public School. Built in 1896, extant, though the building has been under threat of demolition.

The school, designed about 1895 in the offices of Honeyman & Keppie, carries several characteristic Mackintosh details in the decorative treatment of the main entrance, the tall windows, and the internal roof structure of exposed wooden beams and trusses.

Mackintosh's perspective was published in *Academy Architecture,* Vol. 9, 1896, p. 85 and his plans for the school are on p. 80 of the same issue. The drawing is in the University of Glasgow Mackintosh Collection.

Design for Martyr's School. Perspective drawing, 1895. Pen and ink 61.3 × 92.5 cm. (UGMC)

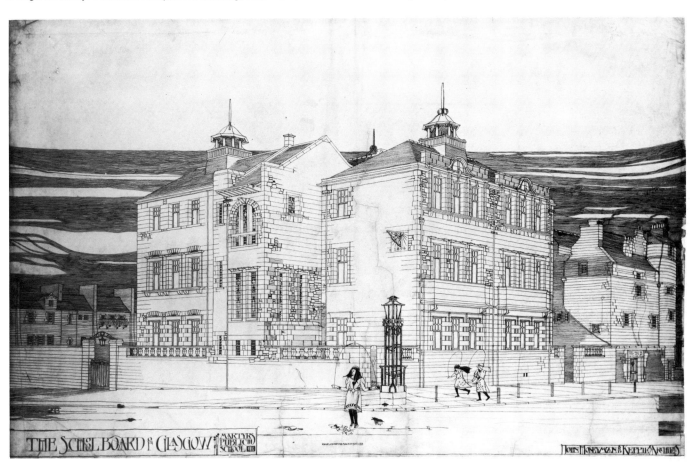

GLASGOW SCHOOL OF ART

167 Renfrew Street, Glasgow

Client: Governors of the School of Art. First phase built 1897-1899; second phase built 1907-1909, extant. The building has been well maintained and continues to function, much according to Mackintosh's design, as a school of art.

While Mackintosh's scheme was at the time condemned as being 'Art Nouveau', and for lacking in classical or historical details such as columns or pediments, the controversial design has since been appreciated as a truly great work of architectural originality, and one of Europe's first buildings in the 'modern style'.

Mackintosh's School of Art, in answer to the Governor's request for a plain building, is an austere statement, a bold breakaway from the traditional methods of architectural adornment. Built of masonry and brickwork, it occupies a difficult, narrow sloping site. Mackintosh used wrought iron to form structural decorative features, and meticulously detailed every interior and exterior aspect of the building. The asymmetric façades of the four main elevations are each distinctive, while the lofty spaces and excellent lighting of the interior are carefully and most successfully designed.

In 1897 Mackintosh revised his design for the second phase of the building, which includes the famous library. His practice of making design alterations while construction proceeded was consistent with his view that drawings indicated an intentional design framework, and were not final or immutable.

View from the North-West. (GSA)

Photographs were published in *The Studio,* vol. XIX, 1900, pp.48 et seq. Mackintosh's plans and drawings are held by the Glasgow School of Art.

THE GLASGOW SCHOOL OF ART.

ELEVATION TO RENFREW STREET

SCALE OF

4 BLYTHSWOOD SQUARE
GLASGOW NOVEMBER 1910

Left — Glasgow School of Art, design for North elevation, 1910. Pencil, ink and watercolour 61 × 91.5 cm. (UGMC)

Below left — Detail of iron screen, North facade. (GSA)

Below — Main entrance on Renfrew Street. (Annan)

Above — West wing, view from the South-West. (Annan)

Above right — East wing. The two large windows on the right, at street level, are later additions. (GSA)

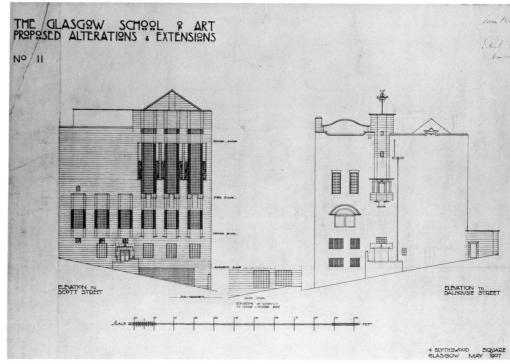

Right — Glasgow School of Art, design for proposed alterations and extensions, East and West elevations, 1907. Pencil and ink 61 × 91.5 cm. (GSA)

THE GLASGOW SCHOOL of ART.

Above — South elevation, contemporary photograph. (GSA)

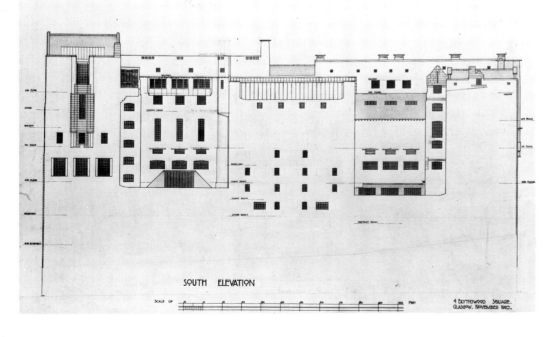

SOUTH ELEVATION

Left — Glasgow School of Art, drawing of South elevation, 1910. Pencil, ink and watercolour 61 × 91.5 cm. From a set made in 1910 of the completed building. (UGMC)

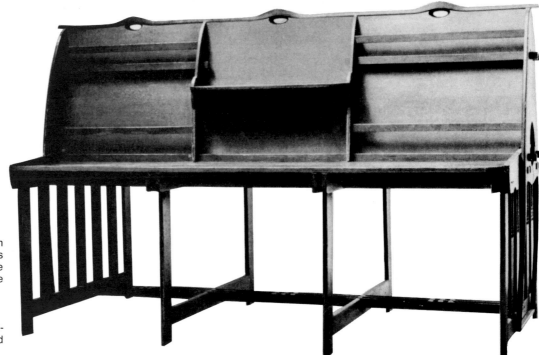

Right — Periodical table from the library. Originally made as a centre table in 1909, the centre screen and racks were later additions. (GSA)

Below — The library. Contemporary photograph by Bedford Lemere. (UGMC)

Above — View from the library gallery towards the entrance. (GSA)

FACING PAGE
The library. (GSA)

Left — The main staircase, leading up to the Museum. (UGMC)

FACING PAGE
The museum, on the first floor. (UGMC)

Below left — Detail of the wrought iron emblem overhanging the stair well.

Below centre — Ogee-shaped ceiling lights and timber strapping in the east corridor.

Below — The West corridor, leading to the Library, with alcove window seats on the left. (UGMC)

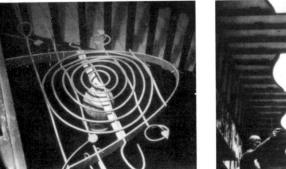

GLASGOW SCHOOL OF ART

Right — The pavilion corridor or 'hen-run', looking West to the loggia. (GSA)

Far right — One of the eight board room pilasters, each one of which is different in detail. (GSA)

The loggia, at the end of the pavilion corridor on the second floor of the West wing. (UGMC)

Above — One of the three identical board room light fittings in wrought iron, with copper shades. (GSA)

Left — The board room.

QUEEN'S CROSS CHURCH

866 Garscube Road, Glasgow
Built 1898, opened in 1899. The church now houses the Charles Rennie Mackintosh Society.

Mackintosh designed this church — a Honeyman & Keppie commission — in 1897, shortly after finishing the Glasgow School of Art Competition drawings. Regarded as one of his less striking designs, the church, which is sited on a busy junction, combines Gothic and Art Nouveau features in an otherwise traditional building of simple plan. Inside, the arched, black-stained timber ceiling and exposed roll steel tie beams and rivets are unusual decorative structural features. The effect of the interior is spacious and restful.

Mackintosh's design for the tower is derived from a parish church he had previously seen and sketched at Merriot in Somerset. The fine oak pulpit, with its carved stylised floral motif and green plush upholstery, the communion table, three chairs, and a cabinet were also designed by Mackintosh.

Perspective published in *Academy Architecture,* XIII, 1898. p.65. Mackintosh's perspective is in the University of Glasgow Mackintosh Collection.

Design for St. Matthews Church (now Queen's Cross). Perspective drawing, 1897. Pencil, pen and ink 56 × 61.8 cm. (UGMC)

St MATTHEWS CHURCH : GLASGOW

: NOW QUEEN'S CROSS CHURCH :

CHARLES R. MACKINTOSH : F.R.I.B.A

JOHN HONEYMAN AND KEPPIE
ARCHITECTS
H. OATH STREET : GLASGOW.

Left — Detail of stonework. (Benton)

Below — Queen's Cross Church. (Annan)

RUCHILL STREET CHURCH HALLS

24 Ruchill Street, Maryhill, Glasgow
Client: Westbourne Free Church. Built 1898 or 1899, extant and in poor condition until recently cleaned and restored.

Mackintosh designed this 2-storey rough-cast and grey sandstone building about 1896. It contains two halls, a committee room, a small store, offices and toilets, and is regarded as a well-planned but minor work.

Only preliminary sketches exist, which are in the University of Glasgow Mackintosh Collection.

Ruchill Street Church Halls, court entrance. (Benton)

WINDYHILL

Kilmacolm, Renfrewshire

Client: William Davidson junior. Building commenced in 1900 and was completed in 1901. The house was altered by subsequent owners, but the present owner has done much to restore the building to its original condition.

Windyhill was designed in 1899, was the first of Mackintosh's private houses and an independent commission. The house, built on an open and steep site at the top of a hill, is surrounded by wide views. Traditional references are evident in the pitched roofs and stern rough-cast masonry walls, yet the house is unmistakably of the 20th century. Much of the furniture designed for the house by Mackintosh in 1901 was later presented to the Glasgow School of Art by the Davidson family.

Photographs of Windyhill and other projects were published in *Dekorative Kunst,* V, March 1902, pp.193-203, 'Die Glasgower Kunstbewegung' by Hermann Muthesius and in Muthesius' *Das Englische Haus,* Vol. 1, pp.185-187, vol. III, pp.98, 172, 214. Perspective drawings are in the Glasgow School of Art.

Windyhill, view from the North. (Annan)

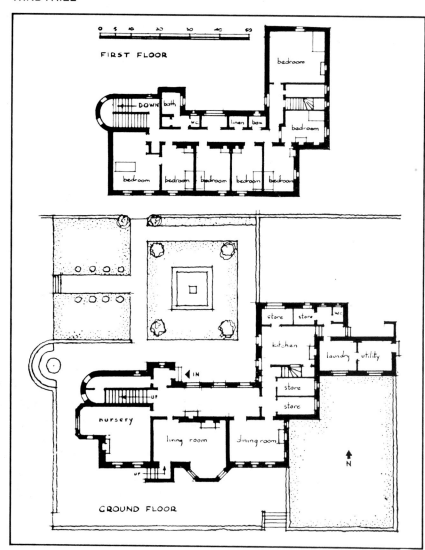

FIRST FLOOR

GROUND FLOOR

Above — The hall fireplace. (UGMC)

Above — Windyhill, ground and first floor plans, 1900. (GSA)

FACING PAGE

Top — The entrance hall. (Annan)

Bottom — The entrance hall. (Annan)

Right — Detail; main entrance. (Annan)

WINDYHILL

Right — Dressing mirror, made for Windyhill as part of the same suite as the wash stand. Oak, painted white enamel. (GSA)

Below — Wash stand, made in 1900 for Windyhill as part of a suite of bedroom furniture. Oak, painted white enamel. (GSA)

Right — Toy chest, made in 1900 for Windyhill. Dark stained oak. (GSA)

Below — Bay window and seating. (Annan)

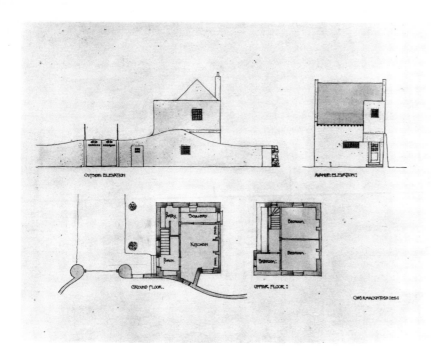

GATE LODGE. AUCHENBOTHIE

Kilmacolm, Renfrewshire
Client: H. B. Collins. Built 1901, extant.

Mackintosh presented at least four design schemes for this curious little four-roomed, square gate-house, attached to the manor, Auchenbothie. The walls are very thick and roughly rendered, the small windows are deep set, and the steep pitch of the pyramid roof rises into a large chimney-stack.

Drawings are in the University of Glasgow Mackintosh Collection.

Above left – Design for Gate Lodge at Auchenbothie, 1901. Pen and wash on cream paper 33.9 × 43.3 cm. (UGMC)

Left – Design for Gate Lodge at Auchenbothie, 1901. Pen, wash and pencil on cream paper 35.5 × 52.8 cm. (UGMC)

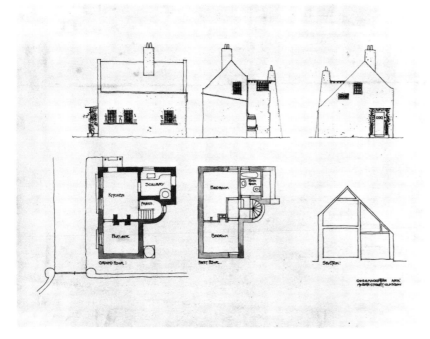

Below left Design for Gate Lodge at Auchenbothie, 1901. Pen and wash on cream paper 33.5 × 43.3 cm. (UGMC)

Below Final design and plan for Gate Lodge at Auchenbothie, 1901. Pen, wash and pencil on cream paper 52.7 × 68.4 cm. (UGMC)

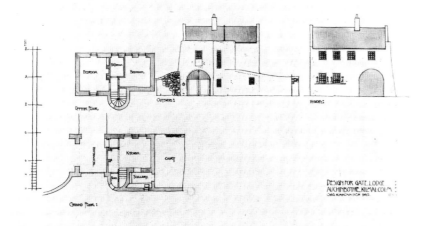

DAILY RECORD BUILDING

Renfield Lane, Glasgow

Client: 'Daily Record' newspaper. Built 1901, extant, though it has undergone alterations and change of use to a warehouse.

This is a large building, the major part being five storeys high and the remainder two storeys high. The site fronts straight onto a narrow lane surrounded by tall buildings and is in constant shadow. Mackintosh skilfully handled the façade, which at ground level is in grey sandstone, rising to the fourth floor in white glazed bricks, with an attic storey in red sandstone.

Only one perspective remains, this being in the University of Glasgow Mackintosh Collection.

Design for the Daily Record Building. Perspective drawing, 1901. Pencil, ink and watercolour 117 × 37.2 cm. (UGMC)

HILL HOUSE

Helensburgh, Dunbartonshire

Client: W. W. Blackie. Built between 1902 and 1903, occupied in 1904. Extant and unchanged, though the Royal Incorporation of Architects in Scotland is fighting to raise funds for the house's preservation and maintenance.

Hill House, the largest and finest of Mackintosh's domestic buildings, was designed in 1902. It occupies a hillside site which looks out over the Clyde estuary, and is surrounded by grounds meticulously landscaped by Mackintosh, who went to the extent of instructing that the trees be clipped according to his manner of drawing them.

Built from local sandstone and rough-cast rendered, the house bears the image of Scottish baronial traditions. For the interior, Mackintosh designed fireplaces, furnishings and fittings. His attentions extended from the design of built-in wardrobes for the white bedroom to the detailing in a superb set of pewter fire tongs and poker. Walls in the house were generally white, some with delicate stencil designs in pale greens, pinks, and silver.

An article and photographs were published in *Deutsche Kunst und Dekoration,* VI, No. 1, March 1905, pp. 337-368, 'The Hill House, Helensburgh' by Fernando Agnoletti.

Plans and photographs of façades and interiors appeared in *Academy Architecture,* 1906, pp.73-75. Perspectives and photographs were published in *The Studio Year-Book of Decorative Art,* 1907, pp.32-33. Some of Mackintosh's drawings for Hill House are in the Glasgow School of Art, others are owned by the Royal Institute of Scottish Architects. An elevation from the South, plan of the principal bedroom and a design for wall decoration are in the University of Glasgow Mackintosh Collection.

FACING PAGE

Top — Hill House. Perspective drawing, 1903. Pen and ink 33.6 × 57.2 cm. (GSA)

Bottom — View from the South-West. (RCAM)

Below — View from the South-East. (RCAM)

VII

VIII

X

Above — View from the West. (RCAM)

Right — Hill House, while under construction. (Annan)

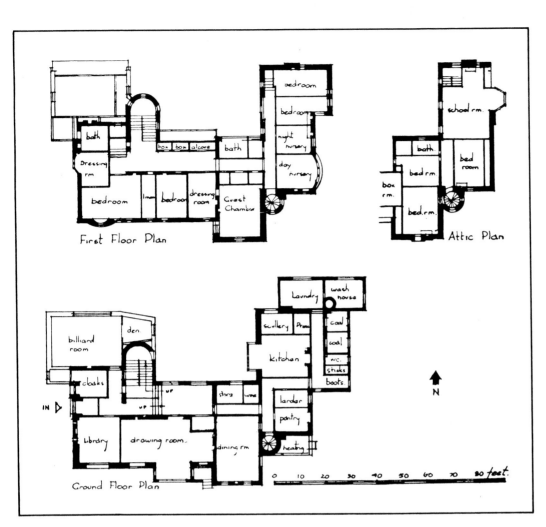

First Floor Plan

bath
Dressing rm
bedroom
bedroom
dressing room
Guest Chamber
box box alcove
bath
bedroom
bedroom
night nursery
day nursery

Attic Plan

school rm.
bath.
bed rm.
bed room
box rm.
bed.rm.

Ground Floor Plan

billiard room
den.
cloaks
Library
drawing room.
dining rm
store
wine
larder
pantry
heating
Laundry
wash house
scullery
Press
coal
coal
w.c.
sticks
boots
kitchen

IN

N

0 10 20 30 40 50 60 70 80 *feet*.

Below left — Detail: main entrance. (Benton)

Below — Detail: exterior of the master bedroom. (Benton)

43

Left — Window and seating, with stencilled rose motif. (RCAM)

Below — The main bedroom. (Annan)

SCOTLAND STREET SCHOOL

Scotland Street, Glasgow

Client: Govan School Board. Built between 1904 and 1906, extant. Minor modifications have been made.

The School, a commission for the firm Honeyman, Keppie & Mackintosh, was designed by Mackintosh in 1903 within the stringent limitations of school board costing. A co-educational school, it required two separate main entrances and suggested a symmetrical plan. Built of red sandstone and reaching to three storeys, it contains twenty-one classrooms. A horizontal line is emphasised in the placement of twin staircase bays at each extremity.

Mackintosh created airy interiors and used simple white glazed tiling to face walls and piers. Still in use for its original purpose, the School is recognised as one of Mackintosh's most attractive buildings. It is owned by the Corporation of Glasgow which has undertaken to preserve it.

Perspective and plans were published in *Academy Architecture,* XXIX, 1906, pp.76-77. Plans, photographs and a description were published in *The Builder's Journal and Architectural Engineer,* XXIV, 28 November 1906, pp. 266-269. A perspective and copies of preliminary plans are in the University of Glasgow Mackintosh Collection.

Detail: staircase bay. (Benton)

FACING PAGE

Detail: interior roof structure. (Benton)

Design for Scotland Street School. Perspective drawing, 1904. Ink on cream paper 54.2 × 110.2 cm. (UGMC)

SCHOOL BOARD ₰ GLASGOW SCOTLAND STREET PVBLIC SCHOOL.

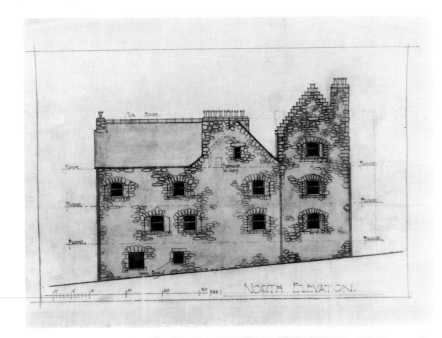

MOSSIDE LATER CLOAK

Near Kilmacolm, Renfrewshire
Client: H. B. Collins. Built 1906, extant. Various alterations, including the reshaping of the roof, have been made by a subsequent owner.

Mosside, which was not, apparently, built according to the original design which incorporated a tower, was subsequently altered by Mackintosh in 1912. Sited on the slope of a loch, Mosside is a large house, unmistakably Scottish with its thick rubble walls, crowstepped gables and slate roof. The exterior is of a severe and rugged appearance, while inside Mackintosh has created lofty, well-proportioned rooms, each with its own fire-place. Perhaps as a result of restrictions on Mackintosh's freedom in this project, Mosside is unlike any other of his domestic designs.

Drawings are in the University of Glasgow Mackintosh Collection.

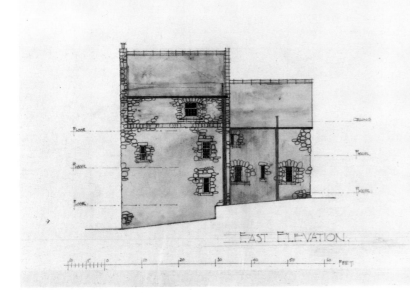

Above left — Mosside, design for North elevation, 1906. Pencil and wash on brown tracing paper 26 × 37 cm. (UGMC)

Left — Mosside, design for East elevation, 1906. Pencil and wash on brown tracing paper 26.7 × 37 cm. (UGMC)

Below left — Mosside, design for South Elevation, 1906. Pencil and wash on brown tracing paper 27 × 37 cm. (UGMC)

Below — Mosside, from the South-West. (Howarth)

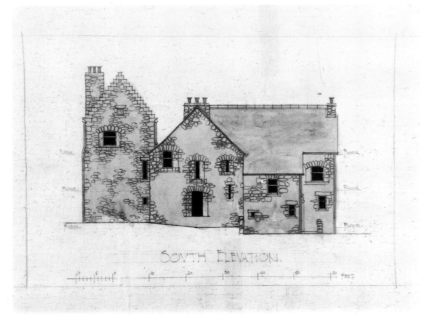

AUCHENIBERT

Near Killearn, Stirlingshire
Client: F. J. Shand. Built 1906, extant.

Auchenibert, designed in 1904, is characterised by a Tudor aspect, differentiating it from Mackintosh's other designs. This presumably reflects the predilections of the Shands, who were later to employ another architect to complete the commission in place of Mackintosh.

The house is built on an attractive rising site, surrounded on three sides by trees. The outside masonry is clean and sharp, in contrast with the rough-hewn quality characteristic of many of Mackintosh's buildings.

A perspective is in the University of Glasgow Mackintosh Collection.

Auchenibert, East front. (Norton)

STUDIO HOUSE, CHELSEA

Glebe Place, Chelsea, London
Client: Harold Squire. Built 1920, extant.

In 1920 Mackintosh was commissioned to design several studios in Chelsea, where he and Margaret Macdonald Mackintosh were now living. Only one of the projects was built — the studio house for the artist Harold Squire — and even this was realised in a manner far removed from the architect's original scheme. Mackintosh had designed for the long narrow site a three-storey building topped with a roof-garden, but this proposal being enormously costly, the design was heavily pruned and a revised scheme built.

Drawings for Mackintosh's unbuilt design for the original three studio houses are owned by Mr. and Mrs. H. Jefferson Barnes and the University of Glasgow Mackintosh Collection.

Design for three Chelsea studios, elevation to Glebe Place, 1920. Only the middle building for Harold Squire was built. Pencil and watercolour on light brown paper 27.6 × 37.2 cm. (Jefferson Barnes)

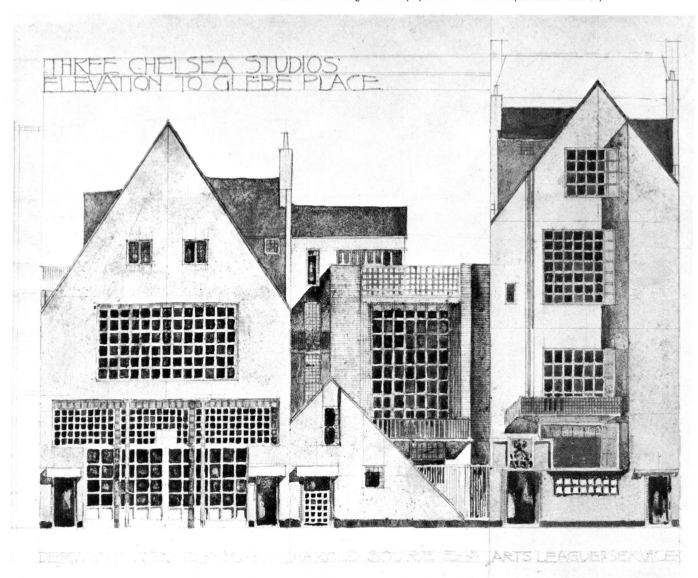

COMMISSIONS
FOR
INTERIORS
AND
ALTERATIONS

GLADSMUIR

Kilmacolm, Renfrewshire
Client: William Davidson senior and family. Nothing remains of this early work.

Between 1894 and 1895 approximately, Mackintosh designed single items of furniture, fabrics, and painted some watercolours for the Davidson family, of whom he was a friend.

LENNOX CASTLE INN

Lennoxtown, Stirlingshire

Honeyman & Keppie were commissioned to carry out alterations to an inn in 1895. Judging from the nature of the design it was Mackintosh who undertook this small project, although his involvement was never officially recorded. The building has only recently been demolished.

The drawings are in the University of Glasgow Mackintosh Collection.

Below left — Lennox Castle Inn, plans for alterations, 1895. Ink, pencil and wash on linen reinforced paper 45.8 × 31 cm. (UGMC)

Below right — Lennox Castle Inn, designs for alterations, 1895. Ink, pencil and wash on linen reinforced paper 46.5 × 31.2 cm. (UGMC)

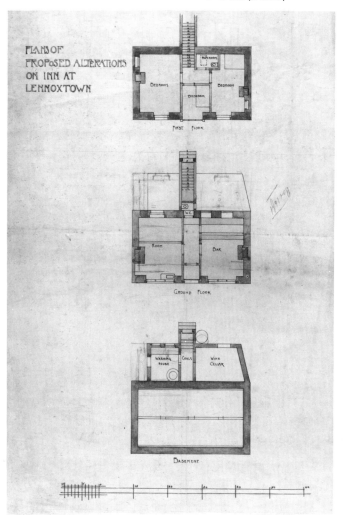

BUCHANAN STREET TEA ROOMS

91-93 Buchanan Street, Glasgow
Client: Miss Catherine Cranston. The Buchanan Street premises, acquired by Miss Cranston in 1895, were remodelled in 1896. The tea rooms were later converted into banking premises, and the interiors completely altered.

George Walton, who was commissioned to redecorate the four floors of tea rooms and dining galleries at Buchanan Street, designed the overall interiors and the various items of furniture. Mackintosh contributed his characteristic highly stylised, stencilled murals in the general dining room, the dinner gallery and the smoking gallery.

An illustrated report by Gleeson White: 'Some Glasgow Designers', appeared in *The Studio,* Vol. XI, No. 51, June 1897, pp.86-100 and 227-236. Three designs of fittings and decoration are in the University of Glasgow Mackintosh Collection.

OVERLEAF

Buchanan Street Tea Rooms. Mural decoration by Mackintosh. (Annan)

Below — Buchanan Street Tea Rooms. Furniture and mural decoration by George Walton. (Annan)

ANNAN. 16106.

ARGYLE STREET TEA ROOMS

114 Argyle Street, Glasgow

Client: Miss Cranston. The premises were acquired in 1892, and remodelled in 1897-98. Few aspects of the original design survived the transition to a shoe shop.

Walton and Mackintosh again collaborated in the remodelling of one of Miss Cranston's famous tea rooms. Professor Howarth has described Argyle Street, with its four floors of amenities, as 'a miniature community centre with a billiards-room, smoking rooms equipped with lounge chairs, and small tables for chess, draughts and dominoes; a reading room, and a separate tea room for ladies.'

George Walton designed the panelling, screens, billiard tables, fireplaces, wall and ceiling decorations, and the electric light fittings. Mackintosh designed the furniture — stools, stocky arm chairs and high ladder-back chairs, tables, coat and umbrella stands. He also furnished both the smoking room and the billiards room.

Mackintosh was commissioned to do the entire design for the Dutch Kitchen which was opened in the basement of Argyle Street in 1906. Meticulously detailed throughout, the room featured a low open-timbered ceiling, painted black, and a colour scheme of black and white with emerald green accents. Alterations were made in the basement during the 1950s, but some of the original design survives.

The Argyle Street Tea Rooms were described and extensively illustrated in *The Studio*, Vol. XXXIX, No. 163, 1906, pp.31-36, 'Modern Decorative Art in Glasgow' by J. Taylor.

Above — One of a series of tables made for the Argyle Street Tea Rooms in 1897. Brown stained oak. (GSA)

Below — Argyle Street Tea Rooms, the Dutch Kitchen. (Annan)

The Dutch Kitchen. (Annan)

DUNGLASS CASTLE

Bowling, Dunbartonshire

Client: the Macdonald family — Margaret Macdonald and her sister Frances, both students at the Glasgow School of Art were, together with Charles Rennie Mackintosh and Herbert McNair, nicknamed 'The Four.' Frances Macdonald married Herbert McNair in 1899, Margaret Macdonald and Mackintosh were married in 1900.

Mackintosh redesigned the drawing-room of Dunglass Castle in 1899. He stripped away the existing ornamental moulding, replaced an old fireplace, and installed an elegant white mantelpiece of great simplicity. A stencilled bird motif was printed onto the linen upholstery, and the family's chairs were re-covered in linen and embroidered.

Dunglass Castle, the drawing-room fireplace. (Howarth)

120, MAINS STREET

Now Blythswood Street, Glasgow

This studio-flat was occupied by the Mackintoshes from the time of their marriage in 1900 until 1906. Everything — from the general interiors down to the cutlery and fire tongs — was designed by Mackintosh and Margaret Macdonald Mackintosh, who contributed to the furnishings and embroideries. The overall effect was of a bare and spacious elegance: white walls, plain grey carpet, natural pine and black-stained furniture, and the dark intimacy of the dining room.

When the Mackintoshes moved to Florentine Terrace, they dismantled fireplaces, fittings and furniture from Mains Street to be reinstalled in their new home.

The Mains Street flat was illustrated in *The Studio*, 1901, special Summer number, pp.110-115, 'Modern British Domestic Architecture'. It was also included in Hermann Muthesius' *Das Englische Haus,* I, pp.186-187. The double wardrobe from Mains Street was illustrated in *Dekorative Kunst*, V, 1902, p.204. Designs for fireplaces are in the University of Glasgow Mackintosh Collection.

Mains Street, the drawing-room. (Annan)

ANNAN. 15395.

Left — The drawing-room. (Annan)

Below — One of a set of eight chairs which first appeared in Mains Street about 1900. Dark stained oak. (GSA)

Above — Oval table made in 1901-1902, which appears in the Mains Street drawing-room. Oak, painted white, with inlaid ivory roses. (UGMC)

Right — One of a pair of bedroom tables made about 1900-1901 for Mains Street. Oak, painted white, with coloured glass inlays and metal handles. (UGMC)

FACING PAGE

Four-poster bed, made about 1900 for the Mains Street bedroom. Oak, painted white, with pink glass panels. (Annan)

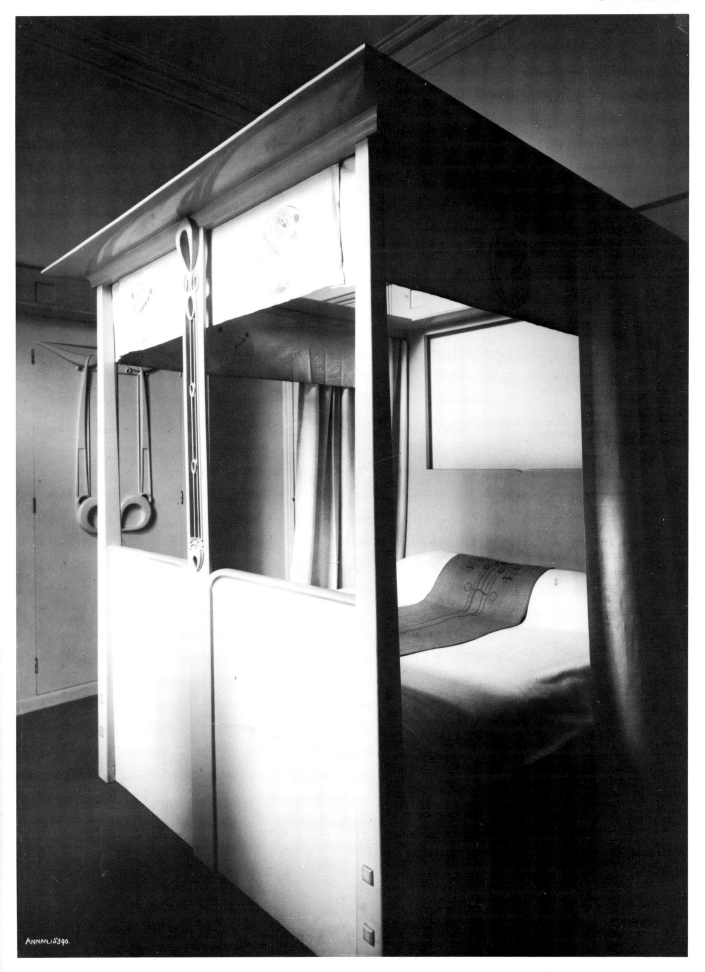

ANNAN. 15390.

34. KINGSBOROUGH GARDENS

Glasgow

Client: Rowat family — Mrs. Newbery, wife of the head of the Glasgow School of Art, was formerly Jessie Rowat.

In 1900 Mackintosh worked on the interiors of the terraced house occupied by the Rowats. He used stencilled motifs on furnishings and walls and created pleasing and uncluttered spaces in primarily white rooms. He also designed the fireplaces and lightfittings.

A photograph of the dining room was reproduced in *Das Englische Haus,* Vol. III, 1904-1905, p.189, by Hermann Muthesius. A design for cabinets and two for wall decorations are in the University of Glasgow Mackintosh Collection.

One of a pair of cabinets designed about 1902 for Mrs. Rowat of Kingsborough Gardens. When they were made it seems that they were kept by the Mackintoshes. Oak, painted white, inside doors painted silver and inlaid with opaque coloured glass. (UGMC)

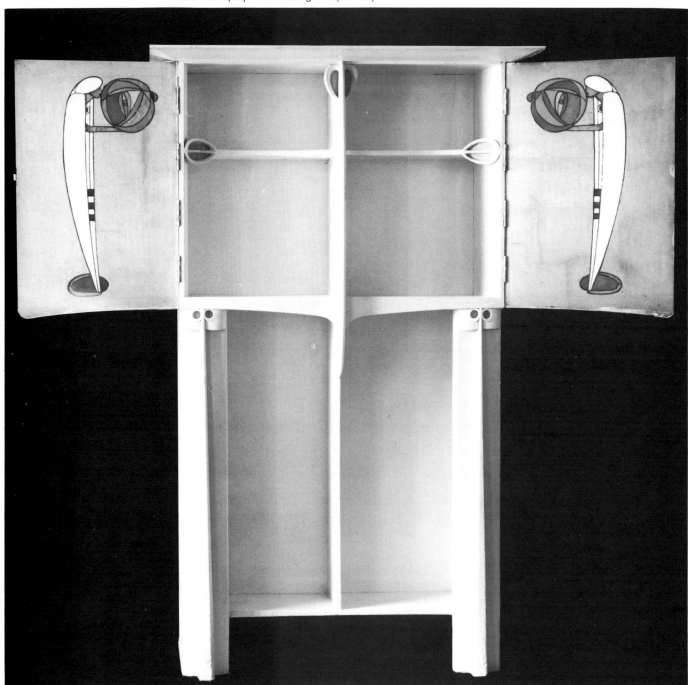

Kingsborough Gardens, the drawing-room fireplace. (From *Das Englische Haus*, 111, p. 189, by Herman Muthesius)

WESTDEL

Queen's Place, Glasgow
Client: J. Maclehose.

Mackintosh designed the interior and furniture for a bedroom and dressing room in about 1900.

The work was illustrated in *Dekorative Kunst,* V, March 1902, pp.208-209, in an article by Hermann Muthesius. Five designs for the bedroom are in the University of Glasgow Mackintosh Collection.

ST. SERF'S CHURCH

Dysart, Fife
Extant, but no traces of Mackintosh's decorative work, c.1900, have been found.

A stencilled mural was illustrated in *Dekorative Kunst,* March, 1902.

INGRAM STREET TEA ROOMS

205-209 Ingram Street, Glasgow

Client: Miss Cranston. The premises were acquired in 1895, and remodelled in 1900-01. In 1950, when the Glasgow Corporation acquired the tea rooms and their fittings, it was expected that Mackintosh's design would be preserved. The building was closed down and the furniture stored. A Scottish 'souvenir' business later leased the premises. The interiors were later (1970) removed and are now in store awaiting re-erection. The premises are now a hotel.

Mackintosh was given control over the entire design for the extension of the tea rooms in 1900. He opened up several walls and put in a new staircase, which, in keeping with the woodwork throughout, was painted white.

Both Mackintosh and his wife produced decorative gesso panels for the tea rooms (these panels were sent in 1902 to be exhibited at the International Exhibition of Modern Decorative Art in Turin).

Left — High-backed chair made in 1907 for the Ingram Street Tea Rooms. Dark stained oak. (GSA)

Below — Ingram Street Tea Rooms, the Cloister Room. (UGMC)

A sketch of the panels was published in *Academy Architecture,* Vol. XX, 1901.

In 1907 The Oak Room was built, a long, narrow, balconied space with an intimate atmosphere. Mackintosh also designed the furniture and cutlery for this room.

In 1911 The Cloister Room was added to the Ingram Street Tea Rooms. It had a low arched ceiling and pine panelled walls and, of course, Mackintosh furniture.

The last room at Ingram Street to be remodelled and furnished by Mackintosh was The China Tea Room, opened in 1911. A geometric motif was used throughout. The walls were lined with coarse hessian and painted blue with wooden lattices. The furniture was dark oak, the upholstery and curtains were in dark blue corduroy.

Designs for furniture and one for a window are in the University of Glasgow Mackintosh Collection.

Below left — Stencilled wall decoration, the Cloister Room. (UGMC)

Below right — The Cloister Room (before alteration). (UGMC)

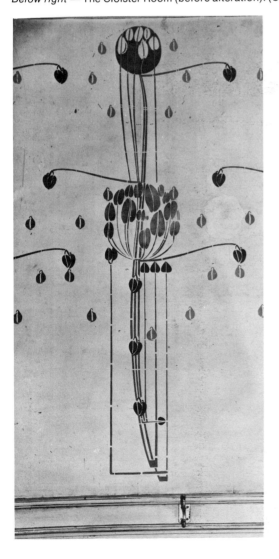

Above — The Chinese Room. (UGMC)

Right — The doorway, Chinese Room. (UGMC)

WARNDORFER MUSIC SALON

Vienna
Client: Mr. and Mrs. Fritz Wärndorfer.

An art patron and one of the founders in 1904 of the Wiener Werkstätte, Wärndorfer shared in the enormous excitement felt in Vienna for Mackintosh's work.

The Music Salon was designed in 1902, Mackintosh having successfully exhibited at Olbrich's Secession House in 1900 and made a firm and positive impression in Austria. Both Mackintoshes collaborated in the work, producing another of the basically white rooms, highlighted with lavender and rose pink tints. Around the walls a frieze of twelve large panels — six painted by Mackintosh and six by Margaret Macdonald — illustrated Maeterlinck's *Dead Princess.* These were probably completed between 1905 and 1907.

The Salon was greatly admired and discussed, and was illustrated in *The Studio,* October, 1912, p.72.

Ultimately the Wärndorfers sold their house and the contents and it seems that the Mackintosh furniture and panels were largely destroyed — although some of the panels were retrieved no trace can be found of them. Photographs of two of the panels are in the University of Glasgow Mackintosh Collection.

Wärndorfer Music Salon. (Howarth)

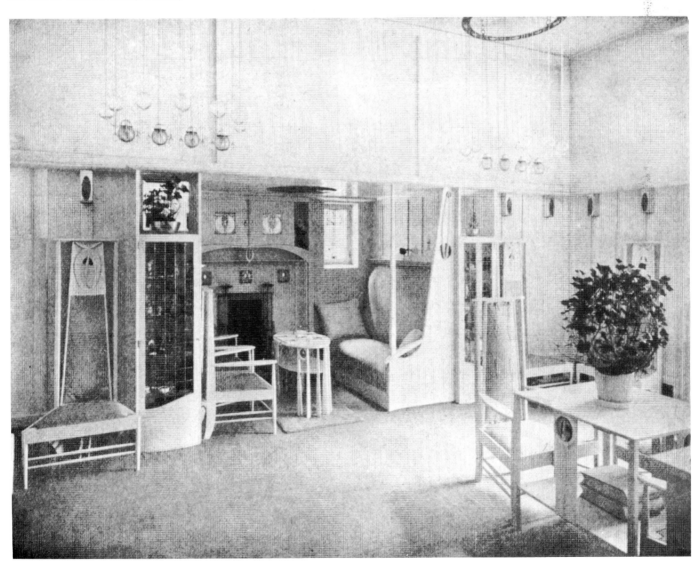

HOUS' HILL

Nitshill, Glasgow
Client: Major and Mrs. John Cochrane. Mrs. Cochrane was formerly Miss Cranston, the restaurateur.

Mackintosh carried out alterations and decorations, beginning about 1903, to this very large and grand old house. The main rooms were completed by 1905, Mackintosh having been solely responsible for the entrance hall, the drawing room, card room, the famous music room, with its curved end wall and open timbered screen, the billiards room and several bedrooms. He also decorated the dining room, and designed various articles of furniture, which co-existed in the house with the Cochrane's collection of antiques.

In 1909 Mackintosh added a highly original and much admired fireplace to the card room and further items of furniture to the house in general.

Hous' Hill was illustrated in *The Studio Year-Book of Decorative Art,* 1907, pp.58-60. The house was demolished in 1933 after a fire, and only a few articles of furniture survive. Some drawings for a wall decoration and the bedroom are in the University of Glasgow Mackintosh Collection.

Above — Hous'hill, the music room. (Annan)

The music room. (Annan)

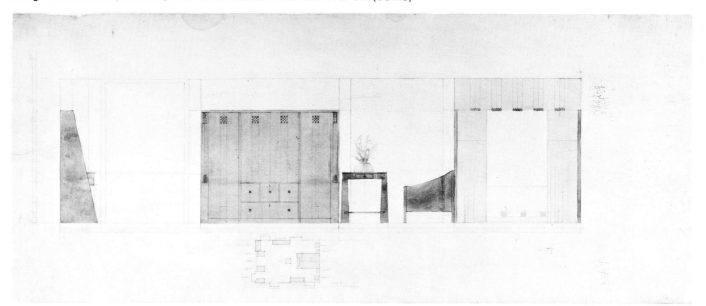

Design for a bedroom, Hous'hill, 1903-1906. Pencil and wash 36.2 × 87 cm. (UGMC)

Design for a bedroom, Hous'hill, 1903-1906. Pencil and wash 36.4 × 87 cm. (UGMC)

Design for a music room, Hous'hill, 1903-1906. Pencil and wash 36.7 × 88.5 cm. (UGMC)

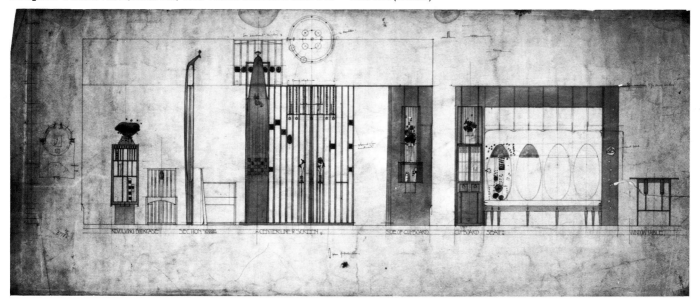

THE WILLOW TEA ROOMS

Sauchiehall Street, Glasgow

Client: Miss Cranston. The site was acquired in 1901 by Miss Cranston, and the new building was completed in 1904. The premises remained in use as tea rooms until the 1920s, when they were incorporated in a store, now Daly's. Although much of the original design has been altered, some aspects remain, and the Room de Luxe is largely intact but bereft of its original furniture.

Mackintosh, the sole architect on this project, was responsible for both the decorative scheme and the structure of the building, which occupies four storeys on a narrow site. The interior consists of various tea rooms, two major dining rooms, a dining gallery, and a timber-panelled billiards room on the top floor. A basement extension designed by Mackintosh — called the Dugout — was added in 1917, and in 1919 he designed for it a memorial fireplace incorporating the flags of the Allies in coloured enamels.

The willow-theme was used as the principal motif throughout the design (Sauchiehall is a Scots word meaning alley of willows). Margaret Macdonald was closely involved in much of the decorative work.

The Room de Luxe, being the most complete and the best known of Mackintosh's tea room interiors, is on the first floor overlooking the street. Its white walls, silver painted high-backed chairs, crisp white tablecloths and blue willow-pattern crockery, soft grey carpet, chairs and settees covered in a rich purple, leaded mirror glass, enamels in pastel pinks and mauves, and the famous leaded-glass doorway, combine to create a glittering elegance, widely celebrated.

An illustrated article on the Willow Tea Rooms was published in *Dekorative Kunst,* VIII, April 1905, pp.257-275, 'Ein Mackintosh Teehaus in Glasgow'. The *Builder's Journal and Architectural Engineer,* 28 November 1906, pp.264-269 showed the building's unusual plain cement façade. A design for the plaster frieze is in the University of Glasgow Mackintosh Collection.

Above — The Gallery Tea Room. (UGMC)

Right — The Dining Room. (UGMC)

Above — The Dining Room. (Annan)

Left — The Dining Room, view from the staircase. (Annan)

THE WILLOW TEA ROOMS

FACING PAGE

Doors to the Room de Luxe, made of leaded mirrored glass. (UGMC)

Right — The Room de Luxe. (UGMC)

Below centre — Chandelier, Room de Luxe. (UGMC)

Below right — Fireplace, Room de Luxe. (UGMC)

Below — Tall clock, made in 1904 for the Willow Tea Rooms. Dark stained oak. (GSA)

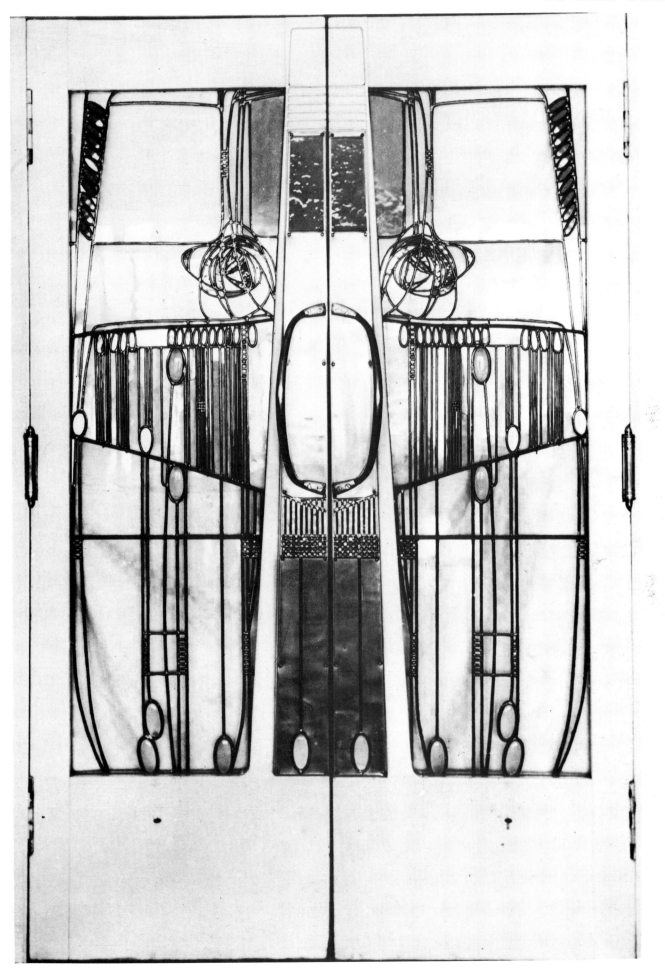

HOLY TRINITY CHURCH

Bridge of Allan, Stirlingshire. *Extant.*

In 1904 Mackintosh designed the pulpit, chairs, organ screen, choir stalls and a very fine communion table which were built from light oak left unstained.

6. FLORENTINE TERRACE

Later 78 Southpark Avenue, Glasgow
The house, acquired by Glasgow University in 1945, was later demolished. However, the University has reconstructed Mackintosh's interiors in an annexe to their new art gallery.

Florentine Terrace — or South Park Avenue — became the Mackintoshes new home in 1906. In his conversion of the terraced house, Mackintosh designed a new front door and, using the furniture and fixtures taken from Mains Street, recreated the colour schemes and the sparse and spacious elegance of their previous apartment.

Plans for alterations, and designs for windows and the drawing room fireplace are in the University of Glasgow Mackintosh Collection.

Left — Florentine Terrace, entrance door. (Annan)

FACING PAGE
The bedroom. (Annan)

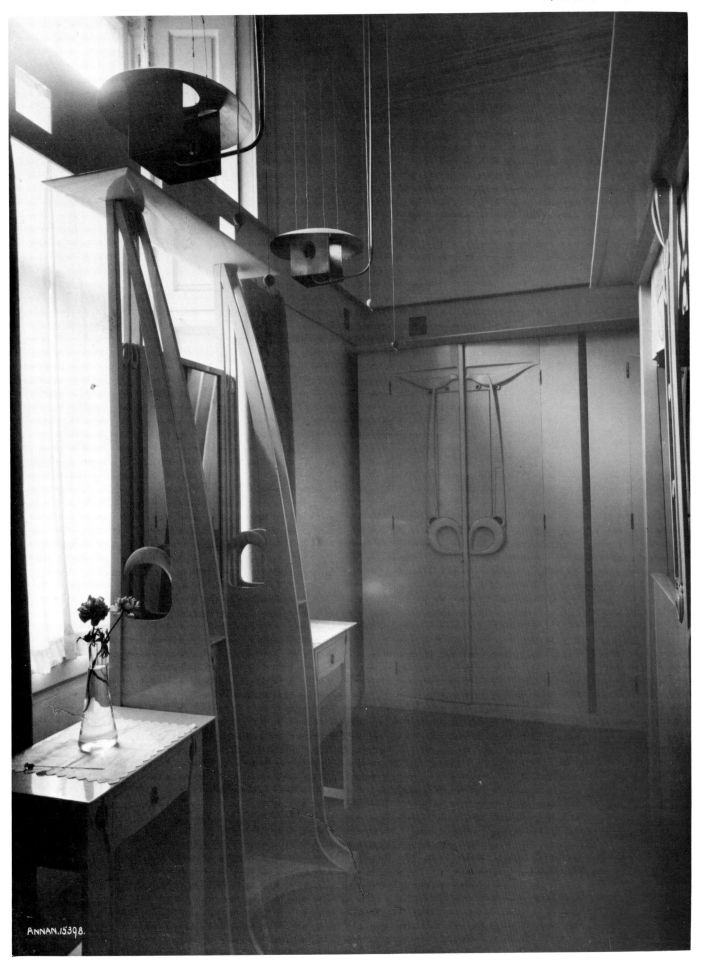

ANNAN.15398.

ABBEY CLOSE CHURCH

Paisley, Renfrewshire. *Demolished.*

A minor ecclesiastical work, dated about 1906, in which Mackintosh designed an organ case, the pulpit and the font. The font is at the Glasgow School of Art.

LADY ARTIST'S CLUB

Blythswood Square, Glasgow. *Extant.*

Mackintosh designed the doorway and interiors of the hall in 1908.

Lady Artist's Club, the doorway. (Scottish Arts Council)

The White Cockade Restaurant during the 1911 exhibition. (Annan)

THE WHITE COCKADE

Miss Cranston's exhibition café at the 1911 International Exhibition in Glasgow.

Mackintosh designed the cutlery, napery and signs for the White Cockade, while Margaret Macdonald designed the menu card. The menu card is in the University of Glasgow Mackintosh Collection.

LADIES HAIRDRESSING SALON

Union Street, Glasgow
Client: Mr. Ritchie. Destroyed.

Mackintosh carried out this minor conversion in 1912. Plans and drawings are in the University of Glasgow Mackintosh Collection.

78.DERNGATE

Northampton
Client: W. J. Bassett-Lowke, extant.

FACING PAGE

Top left — Extension to the garden façade. (UGMC)

Top right — 78 Derngate, entrance door and bay window. (UGMC)

Bottom left — Design for the entrance door to 78 Derngate. Pencil and watercolour 39.2 × 26.9 cm. (UGMC)

Bottom right — The lounge hall fireplace. (UGMC)

Between 1915 and 1917 Mackintosh carried out a commission to completely remodel the exterior and interior of this red brick Victorian terrace house. His conversion shows ingenious planning, most impressively in his handling of the interiors, and in particular the lounge-hall and guest room. Howarth has written of the lounge-hall: 'The walls and ceiling were painted a dull, velvety black and all the woodwork and furniture was stained black and wax polished. The walls were divided into narrow vertical panels by strips of stencilled white chequer pattern. The frieze . . . consisted of nine horizontal bands of small triangular leaf-shaped motifs stencilled golden yellow and outlined in silver grey. These were interspersed by other of vermilion, blue, emerald green and purple, thus giving a rich subdued band of colour right round the apartment.'

Mackintosh also designed furniture for the Basset-Lowke's weekend home, Candida Cottage.

78 Derngate was illustrated in *The Ideal Home,* September 1920. A stencilled frieze designed in 1920 by Mackintosh to replace the original 1916 design used in the lounge-hall was later used in New Ways, the house designed in Northampton for the Basset-Lowkes by Peter Behrens in 1925. Designs for this frieze are in the Royal Institute of British Architects Drawing Collection. Photographs and designs for 78 Derngate are in the University of Glasgow Mackintosh Collection.

Below — The principal bedroom. (UGMC)

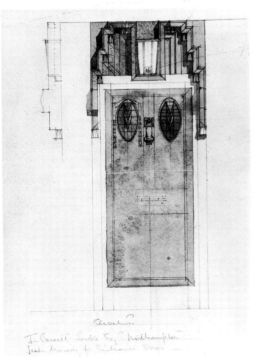

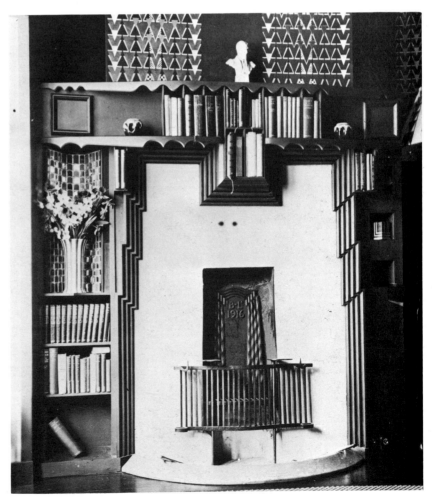

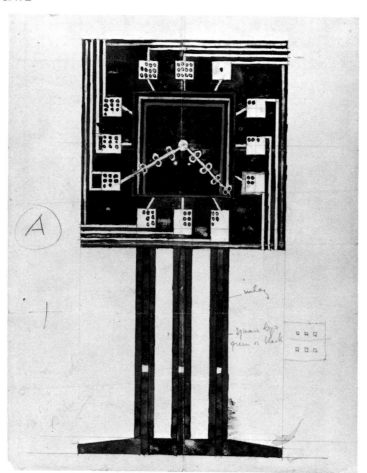

Left — Design for a clock for W. J. Bassett-Lowke of 78 Derngate, 1917. Pencil and watercolour 26.1 × 20.6 cm. (UGMC)

FACING PAGE

The entrance hall. (UGMC)

Below — Scale drawing of staircase screen in the entrance hall, 1917. Watercolour and pencil 34.3 × 51.6 cm (UGMC)

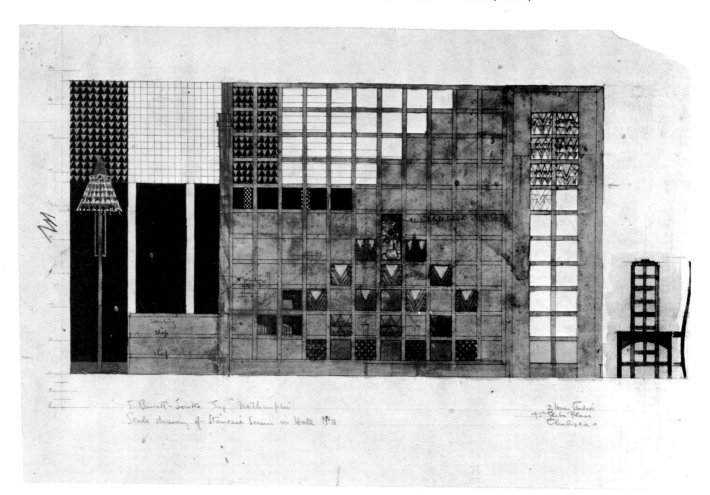

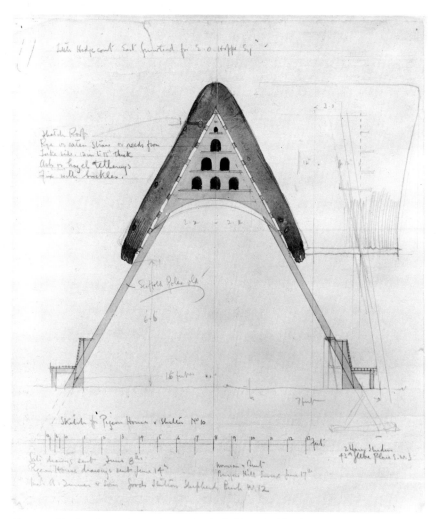

THE DRIVE, NORTHAMPTON

Northampton
Client: F. M. Jones (brother-in-law of Bassett-Lowke).

A small commission, Mackintosh designed the decorations and furniture for one of the rooms in 1917.

COTTAGE, LITTLE HEDGECOURT

East Grinstead, Sussex
Client: E. O. Hoppé. Built in 1919.

An undistinguished and uncharacteristic Mackintosh design, comprising the extensions to a gamekeeper's cottage which was converted into a studio-house for E. O. Hoppé, the famous photographer.

The original drawings are in the University of Glasgow Mackintosh Collection.

COTTAGE, BURGESS HILL

Burgess Hill, Surrey
Client: Miss Brooks, 1920.

It is unknown whether or not this commission was a complete project or involved only minor alterations.

Above — Design for a pigeon house for O. E. Hoppé of Little Hedgecourt. Pencil and watercolour on cream paper 31.6 × 28.1 cm. (UGMC)

Below — The Drive, dining room. (UGMC)

SELECTED
COMPETITIONS
AND
UNEXECUTED
PROJECTS

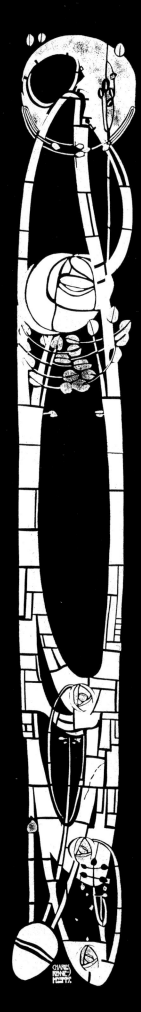

1887

Mackintosh was awarded two prizes by The Glasgow Institute of Architects.

1888

Mackintosh won the Bronze Medal at the South Kensington National Competition for his design, A Mountain Chapel.
The result was published in *Building News*, 1888.
Mackintosh won another Glasgow Institute prize in the same year.

1889

Mackintosh was awarded one of the Queen's Prizes at South Kensington for his design, A Presbyterian Church.
This was reported in *Building News*, 2nd August 1889, p.35.
A cross-section and plan are in the University of Glasgow Mackintosh Collection.

1890

The Glasgow Institute of Architects awarded Mackintosh the Alexander Thomson Travelling Scholarship (£60.00), for his design, A Public Hall. Drawings, perspective and plans were published in *The British Architect*, XXXIX, 28 November 1890, pp.381, 383-385, 406-407.
Drawings for A Public Hall together with another project, A Science and Art Museum, were entered for the South Kensington competition of 1891 for architectural students. Mackintosh won the National Silver Medal with his entry.
Elevation and plans for A Science and Art Museum were illustrated in *The British Architect*, XXXIX, 30 October 1890, pp. 324-325.
An article attacking Mackintosh's design was published in *The Builder*, LXI, 1891, p.81. The original sepia-rendered drawing of the front elevation is in the University of Glasgow Mackintosh Collection.

1891

Mackintosh submitted an unpremiated design, Tenement Buildings, for a competition sponsored by the City of Glasgow Improvement Trust. Drawings are in the University of Glasgow Mackintosh Collection.

1892

Mackintosh submitted his design, A Chapter House, for the Soane Medallion Competition. The Scheme was unpremiated, though commended. An article and illustrations were published in *The British Architect*, XXXVII, 4 March 1892, p.173, 178-179.
The drawings for A Chapter House were submitted later in the year for the South Kensington competition, where they earned for Mackintosh the National Gold Medal.
The results were published in *Building News*, 29 July 1892, p.131.
Mackintosh submitted an unpremiated design for the Glasgow Art Galleries competition.
An article and a perspective were published in *The British Architect*, XXXVII and XXXVIII.

1893

Mackintosh's design for A Railway Terminus, entered for the Soane Medallion Competition, was unpremiated.
An article and front elevation were published in *The British Architect*, XXXIX, 17 February 1893, pp. 118-119, 112. Plans, longitudinal section and elevation, Vol. XXXIX, 24 February 1893, pp.136, 137; cross-section Vol XXXIX, 3 March 1893, p.157.
Drawings are in the University of Glasgow Mackintosh Collection.

1894

Mackintosh worked on the unpremiated design submitted by Honeyman & Keppie for the Royal Insurance Building competition in Glasgow.

1898

Honeyman & Keppie entered the competition for the National Bank of Scotland building in Glasgow. The entry was drawn by Mackintosh, who was probably involved in the design.
The drawings are in the University of Glasgow Mackintosh Collection.
Another unpremiated competition entry by Honeyman & Keppie in 1898 was for the second International Exhibition of 1901 in Glasgow. The firm submitted three designs, one of which was by Mackintosh. Drawings for a Grand Hall, a Concert Hall, and an Industrial Hall are in the Glasgow School of Art and the University of Glasgow Mackintosh Collection.

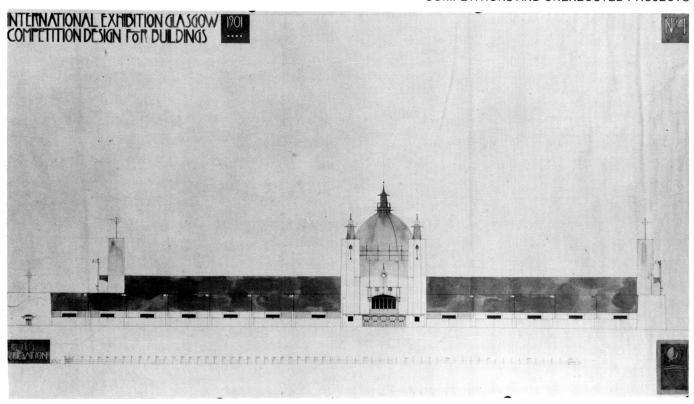

Design for the 1901 Glasgow International Exhibition Buildings Competition. South elevation, 1898. Pencil and wash on cream paper 90.3 × 153.2 cm. (UGMC)

Design for the 1901 Glasgow International Exhibition Buildings Competition. West and East elevations of Industrial Hall, 1898. Pencil and wash on cream paper 90 × 153 cm (UGMC)

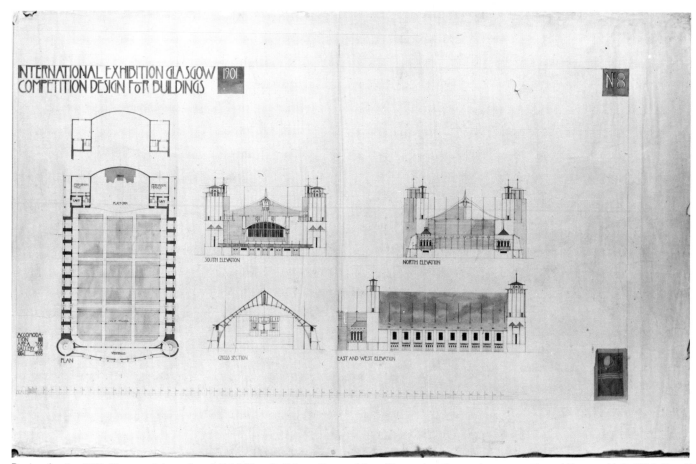

Design for the 1901 Glasgow International Exhibition Buildings Competition. Plans, elevation and cross section of Concert Hall, 1898. Pencil and wash on cream paper 90.3 × 153.2 cm. (UGMC)

Design for the 1901 Glasgow International Exhibition Buildings Competition. Plans for Alternative Concert Hall, Bar and Dining Room, and Bridge, 1898. Pencil and wash on cream paper 90.3 × 148.2 cm. (UGMC)

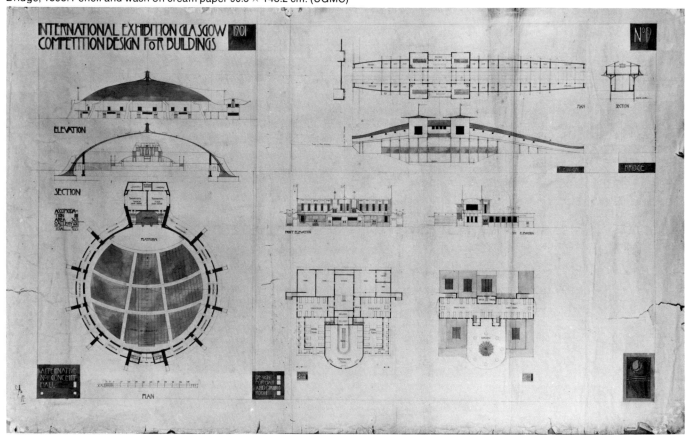

1900

Project for An Artist's Country Cottage and An Artist's Town House. Hermann Muthesius referred to these unexecuted designs by Mackintosh in an article in *Dekorative Kunst,* V, March 1902, pp.211-213.

Mackintosh's drawings for An Artist's Country Cottage are in the University of Glasgow Mackintosh Collection. Drawings for An Artist's Town House are in the Glasgow School of Art.

Unexecuted design for A Country Mansion. One drawing of elevations is in the University of Glasgow Mackintosh Collection.

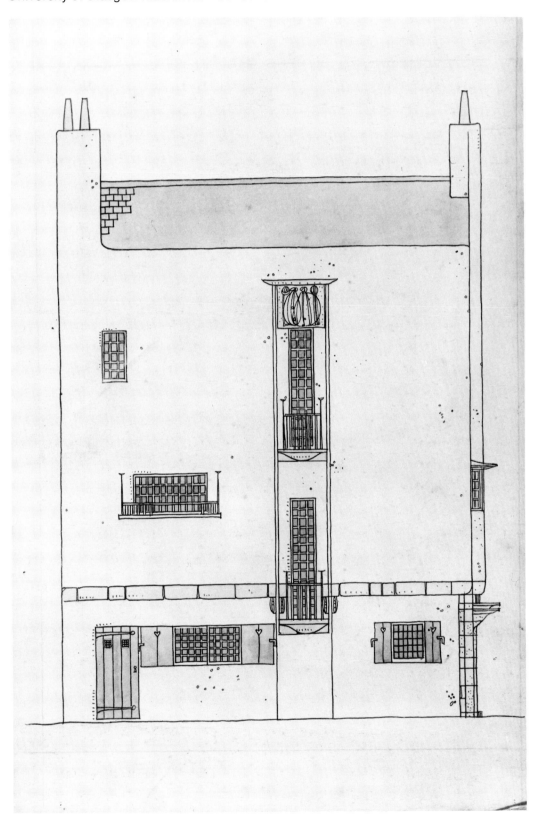

Design for an artist's town house and studio, South elevation, 1900-1901. Pencil, pen and ink and watercolour 39.9 × 27.6 cm. (GSA)

FACING PAGE

Top — Design for an artist's country cottage and studio, South elevation and plan, 1901. Pen, pencil and light green wash on cream paper 20.3 × 44.7 cm. (UGMC)

Bottom — Design for an artist's country cottage and studio, East elevation, 1901. Pen, pencil and watercolour 20 × 24.8 cm. (UGMC)

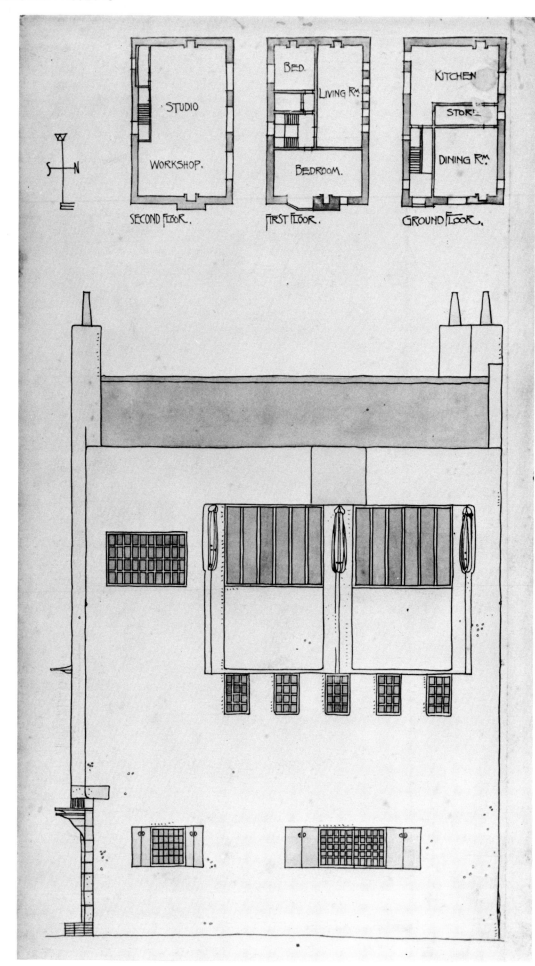

SECOND FLOOR.   FIRST FLOOR.   GROUND FLOOR.

Design for an artist's town house and studio, North elevation and plans. Pencil, pen and ink and watercolour 49.8 × 27 cm. (GSA)

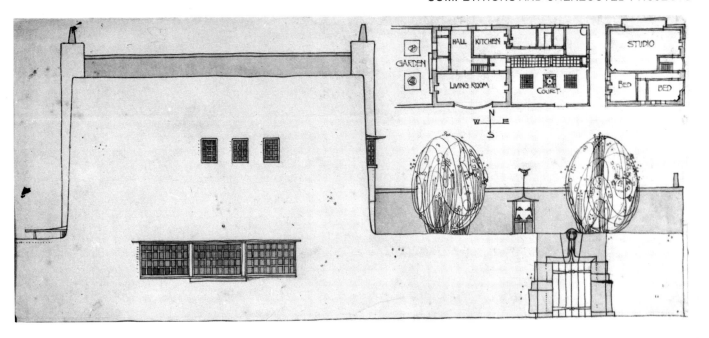

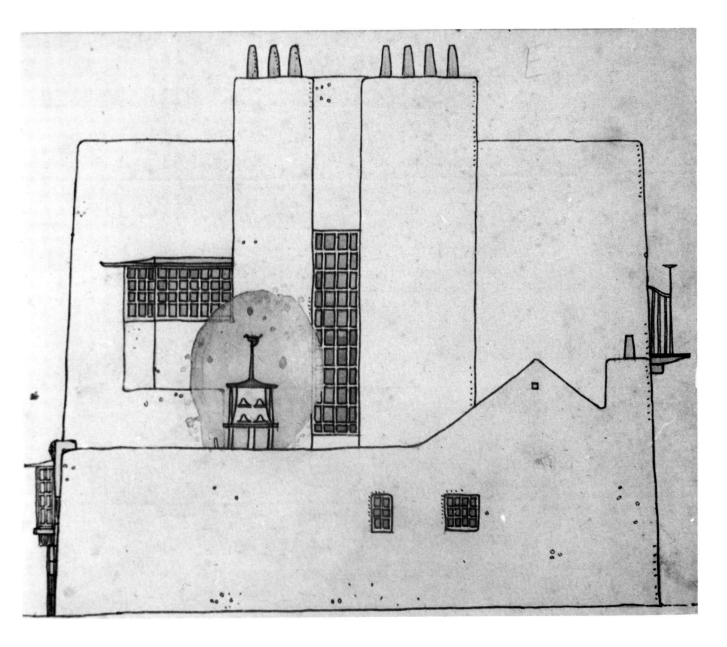

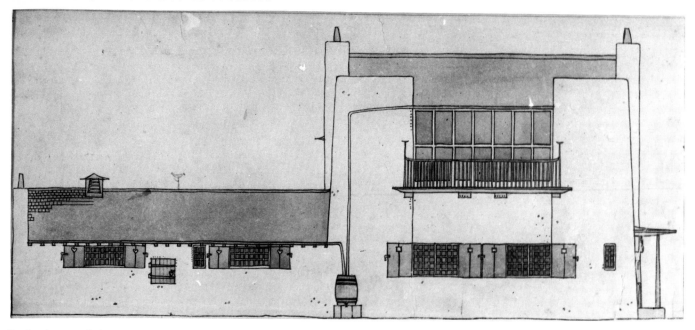

Design for an artist's country cottage and studio, North elevation, 1901. Pencil, pen and ink, and watercolour 20.3 × 44.7 cm. (UGMC)

Design for an artist's country cottage and studio, West elevation, 1901. Pen, pencil and grey and light green wash 20.3 × 25 cm. (UGMC)

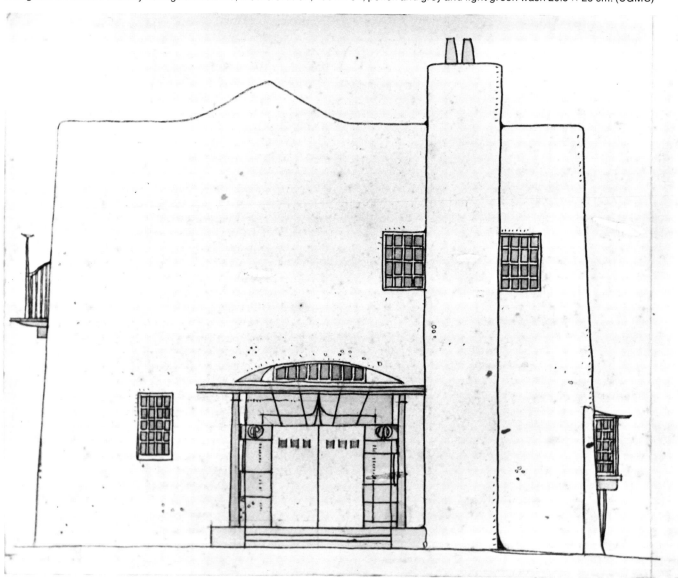

1901

Haus eines Kunstfreundes — house for an art-lover.

Mackintosh entered this unpremiated competition, organised by *Zeitschrift fur Innendekoration*. Although it is widely believed that Baillie Scott won the competition and that Mackintosh came second, the first prize was in fact not awarded, and was instead shared among sixteen of the entrants. Baillie Scott was awarded second prize, and third prizes were given. Mackintosh's entry was disqualified, as his interior renderings were not finished in time for the competition deadline. When they did arrive, however, Mackintosh was awarded a special prize.

Illustrations appeared in *Deutsche Kunst und Dekoration,* Vol II, Book 6, p.516.

Mackintosh's entry scheme for *Haus eines Kunstfreundes* was published in 1902 as a portfolio by Alexander Koch in *Meister der Innenkunst,* with an introduction by Hermann Muthesius. Baillie Scott's entry and that of one of the third-place prizewinners, Bauer, were also published as portfolios.

The drawings are now in the Glasgow School of Art.

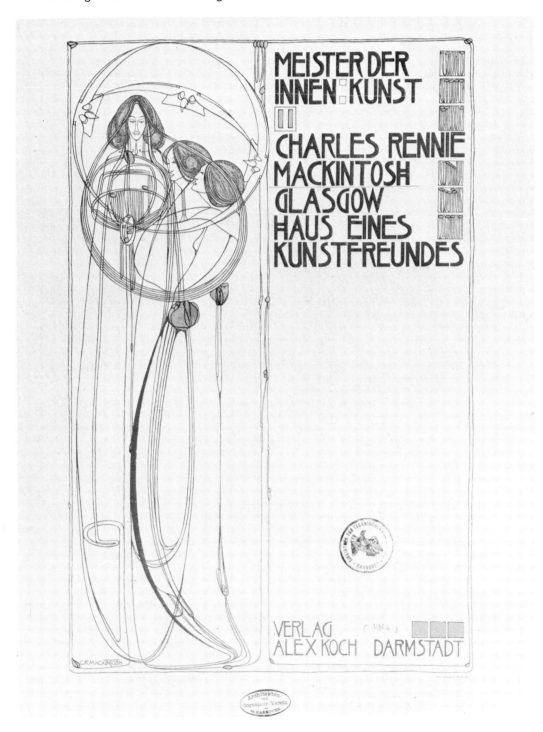

Cover for the lithographic portfolio edition of Mackintosh's entry for the *Haus Eines Kunstfreundes* competition. (UGMC)

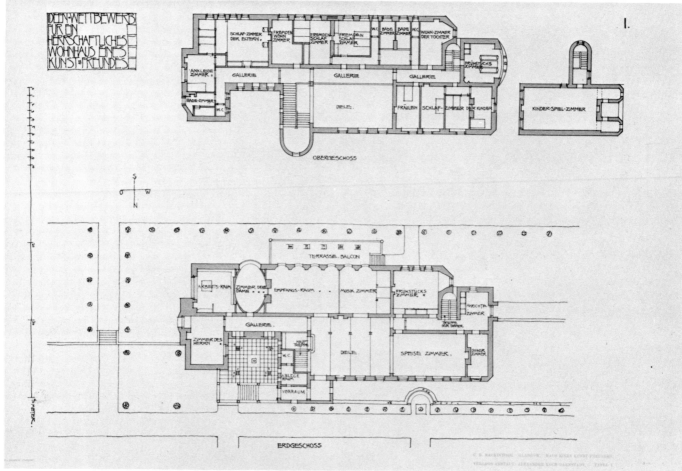

Haus Eines Kunstfreundes, ground and first floor plans, 1901. (UGMC)

Haus Eines Kunstfreundes, design for East and West elevations, 1901. (UGMC)

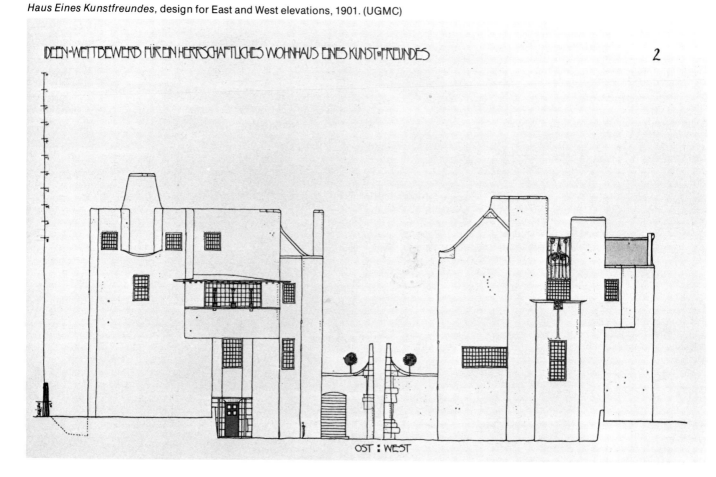

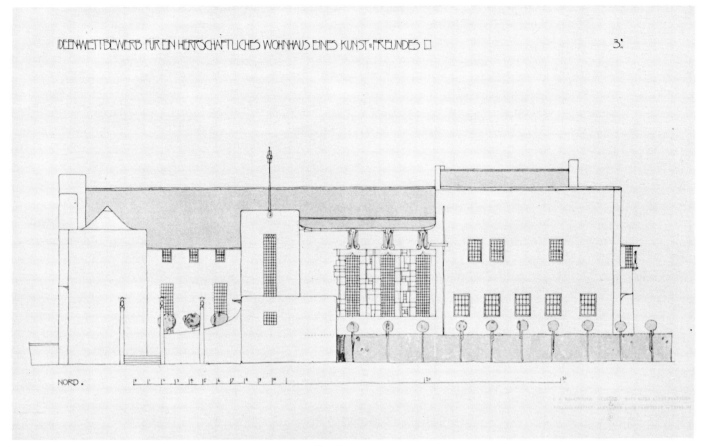

IDEEN-WETTBEWERB FÜR EIN HERRSCHAFTLICHES WOHNHAUS EINES KUNST=FREUNDES ⊡

NORD.

Haus Eines Kunstfreundes, design for North elevation, 1901. (UGMC)

Haus Eines Kunstfreundes, design for South elevation, 1901. (UGMC)

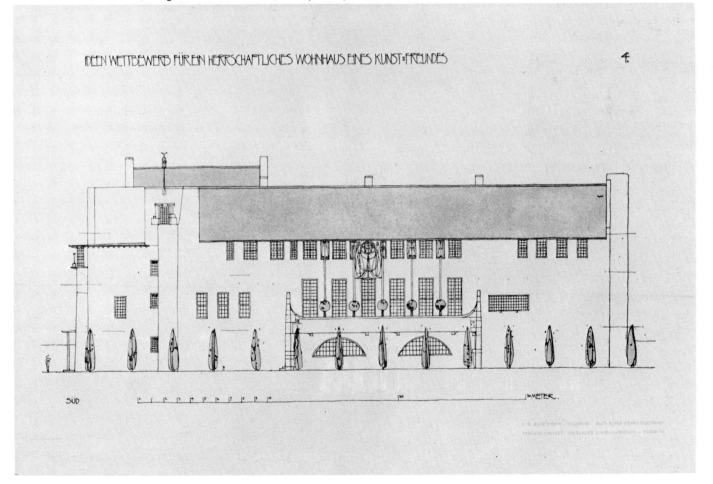

IDEEN WETTBEWERB FÜR EIN HERRSCHAFTLICHES WOHNHAUS EINES KUNST=FREUNDES

SÜD

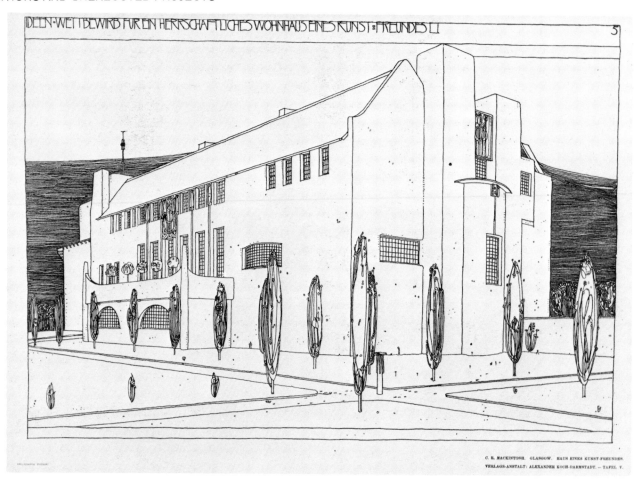

C. R. MACKINTOSH. GLASGOW. HAUS EINES KUNST FREUNDES.
VERLAGS-ANSTALT: ALEXANDER KOCH-DARMSTADT. — TAFEL V.

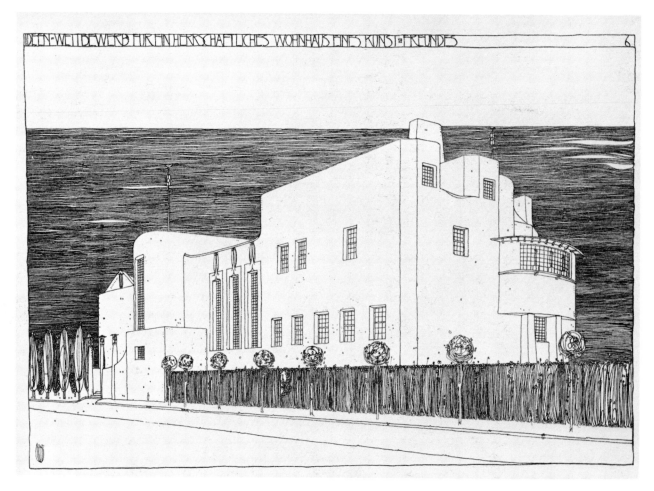

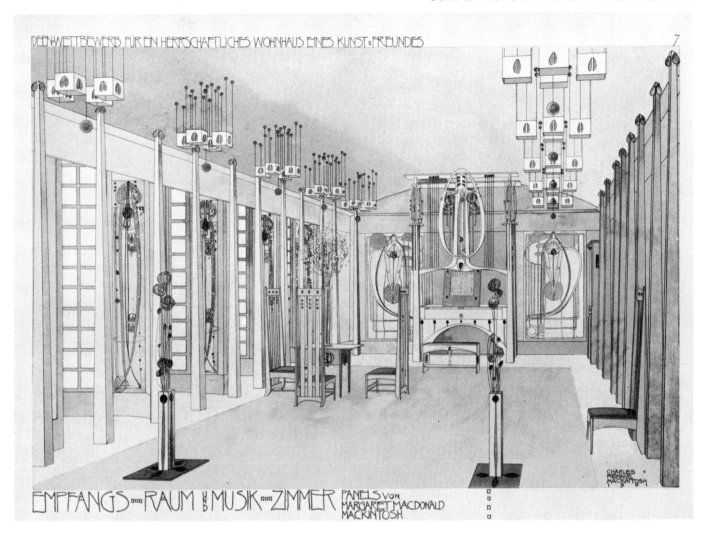

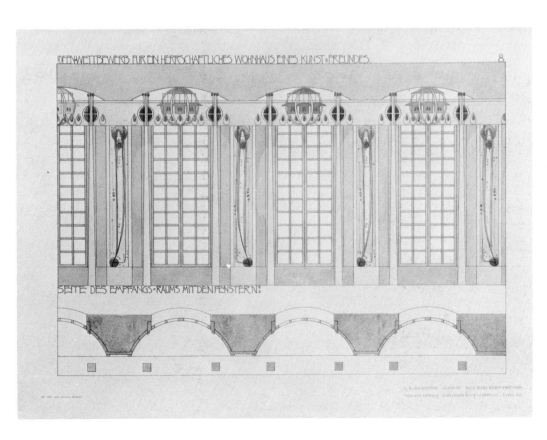

Above — *Haus Eines Kunst-freundes,* design for the music room, 1901. (UGMC)

Left — *Haus Eines Kunst-freundes,* design for the reception room windows, 1901. (UGMC)

FACING PAGE

Top — Design for *Haus Eines Kunstfreundes,* view from the South-East. Perspective drawing, 1901. (UGMC)

Bottom — Design for *Haus Eines Kunstfreundes,* view from the North-West. Perspective drawing, 1901. (UGMC)

FACING PAGE

Top — *Haus Eines Kunstfreundes,* design for the bedroom, 1901. (UGMC)

Bottom — *Haus Eines Kunstfreundes,* design for the entrance hall, 1901. (UGMC)

Right — *Haus Eines Kunstfreundes,* design for the music room fireplace, 1901. (UGMC)

Below — *Haus Eines Kunstfreundes,* design for the nursery, 1901. (UGMC)

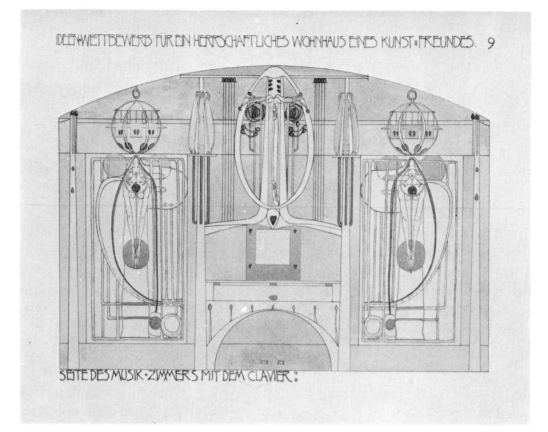

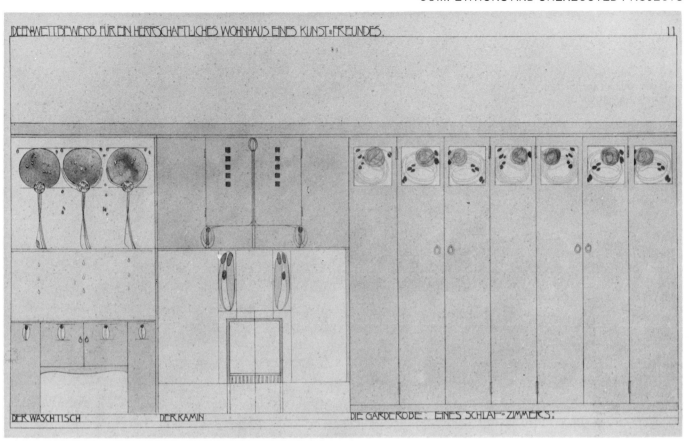

IDEEN=WETTBEWERB FÜR EIN HERRSCHAFTLICHES WOHNHAUS EINES KUNST=FREUNDES.   11

DER WASCHTISCH   DER KAMIN   DIE GARDEROBE: EINES SCHLAF=ZIMMERS:

IDEEN=WETTBEWERB FÜR EIN HERRSCHAFTLICHES WOHNHAUS EINES KUNST=FREUNDES   12:

GALLERIES

DIE DIELE: DIE THÜR DES EMPFANGS=RAUMS: DER KAMIN:

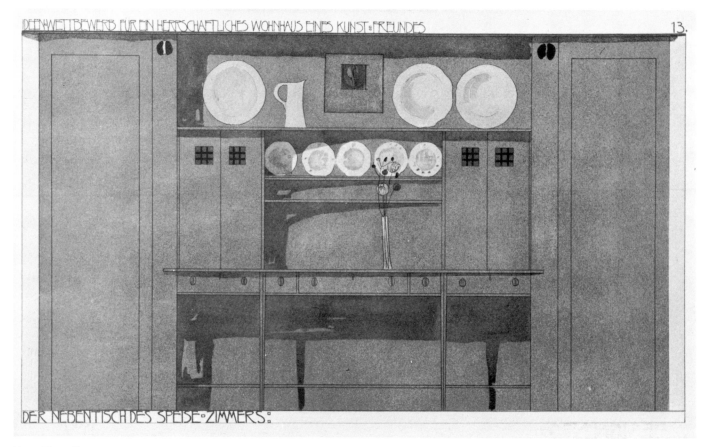

Haus Eines Kunstfreundes, design for the dining room cupboard and shelving, 1901. (UGMC)

Haus Eines Kunstfreundes, design for the dining room, 1901. (UGMC)

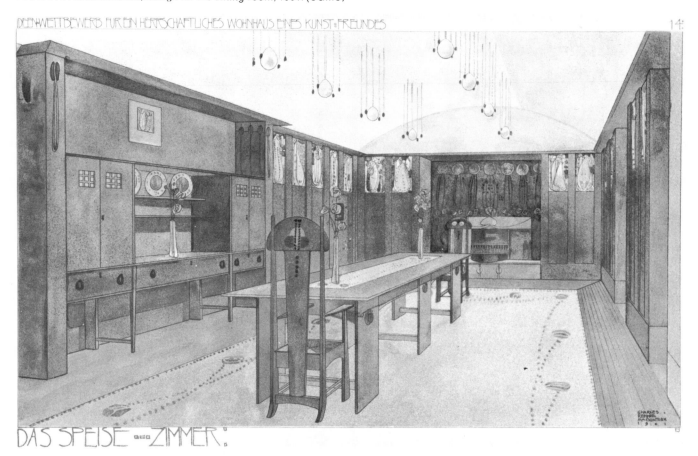

1903

The firm of Honeyman, Keppie & Mackintosh submitted a scheme designed by
Mackintosh for the Liverpool Anglican Cathedral Competition. It was unpremiated,
though drew comment. Giles Gilbert Scott won the commission.
The British Architect, LIX, 13 March 1903, contained an article, pp.190-191, and
drawings on pp.190, 191, 194, 195.
Mackintosh's drawings are in the University of Glasgow Mackintosh Collection.

Design for Liverpool Cathedral, perspective drawing, 1903. (Annan)

DESIGN Nº 2   Nº 7.

PERSPECTIVE   Honeyman Keppie & Mackintosh
                                                   140 BATH STREET GLASGOW

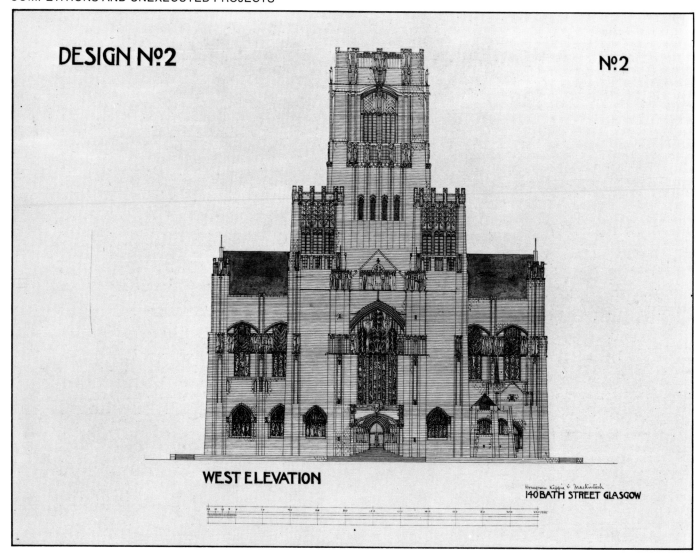

DESIGN N.º2   N.º2

WEST ELEVATION

Honeyman Keppie & Mackintosh
140 BATH STREET GLASGOW

Above — Design for Liverpool
Cathedral, West elevation,
1903. (Annan)

Right — Design for Liverpool
Cathedral, plan, 1903. (Annan)

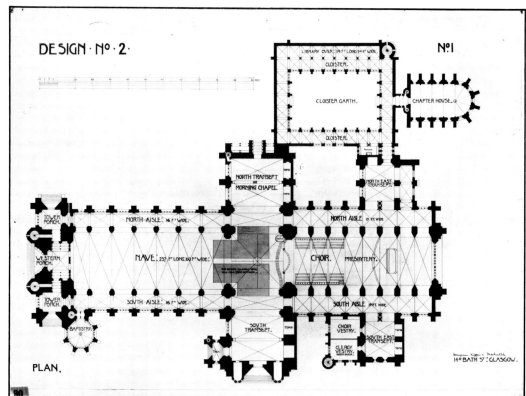

FACING PAGE

Top — Design for Liverpool
Cathedral, South elevation,
1903. (Annan)

Bottom — Design for Liverpool
Cathedral, longitudinal section, 1903. (Annan)

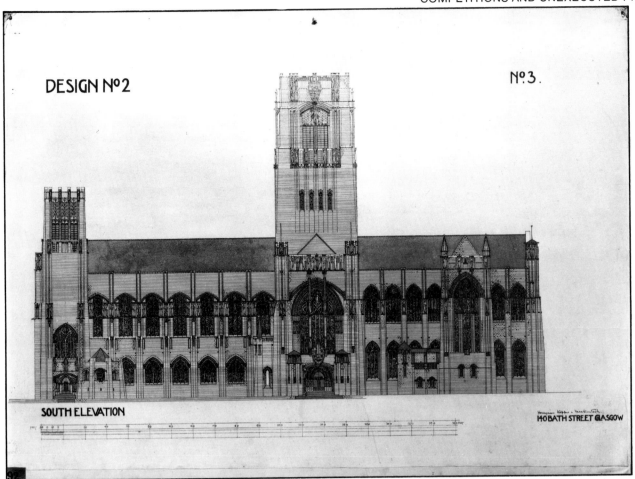

DESIGN Nº 2   Nº 3.

SOUTH ELEVATION   HONEYMAN KEPPIE & MACKINTOSH
                                                  140 BATH STREET GLASGOW

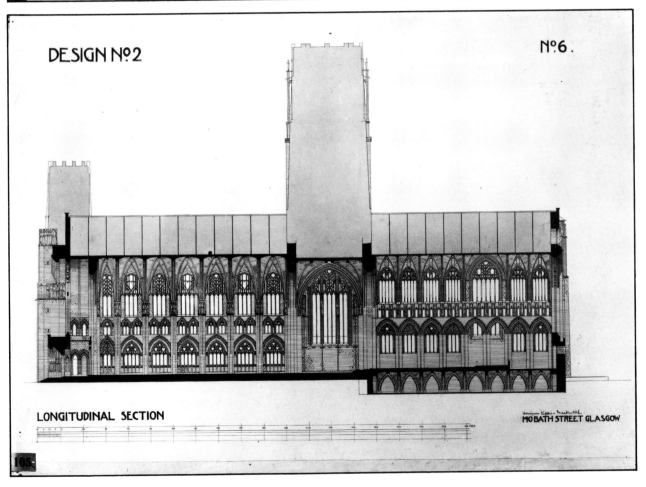

DESIGN Nº 2   Nº 6.

LONGITUDINAL SECTION   HONEYMAN KEPPIE & MACKINTOSH
                                                  140 BATH STREET GLASGOW

1920

Mackintosh designed several schemes for buildings in Chelsea. Various elements, in particular official disapproval of the absence of classical detailing and lack of funds, contributed to the designs being unrealised. Only one studio was built, this being for the artist Harold Squire in Glebe Place.

1920

Proposed studio-house in Chelsea designed by Mackintosh for F. Derwent-Wood, sculptor, and A. Blunt, artist.
Drawings belong to Mr. and Mrs. H. Jefferson Barnes, Helensburgh, Dunbartonshire.

Design for Three Chelsea Studios, elevation to Cheyne House Garden, 1920. Pencil and watercolour on light brown paper 27.6 × 37.2 cm. (Jefferson Barnes)

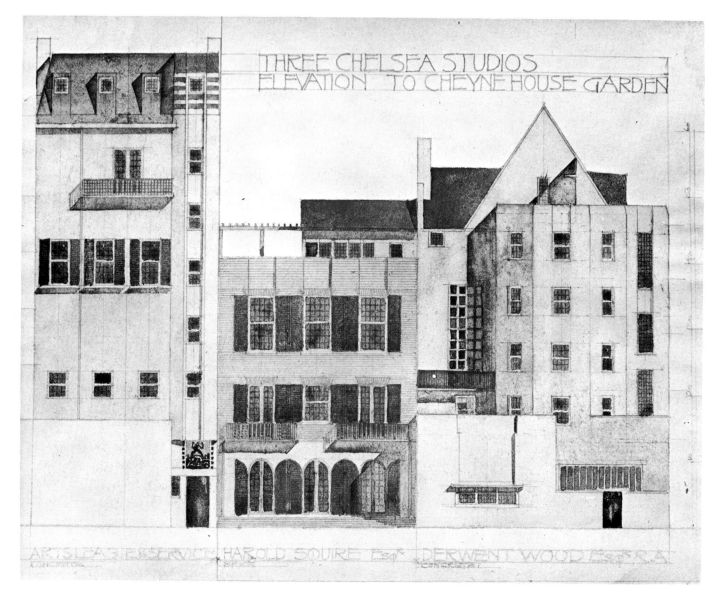

1920

Proposed studio-flats designed for the Arts League of Service in Chelsea. Objections from the local authority were eventually overcome, but not enough money was available to enable the project to be realised. Drawings belong to Mr. and Mrs. H. Jefferson Barnes and the University of Glasgow Mackintosh Collection.

Design for a block of studios for the Arts League of Service. Elevation to Upper Cheyne Row, elevation to Cheyne House Garden, and plan, 1920. Pencil and watercolour on light brown paper 27.6 × 37 cm. (Jefferson Barnes)

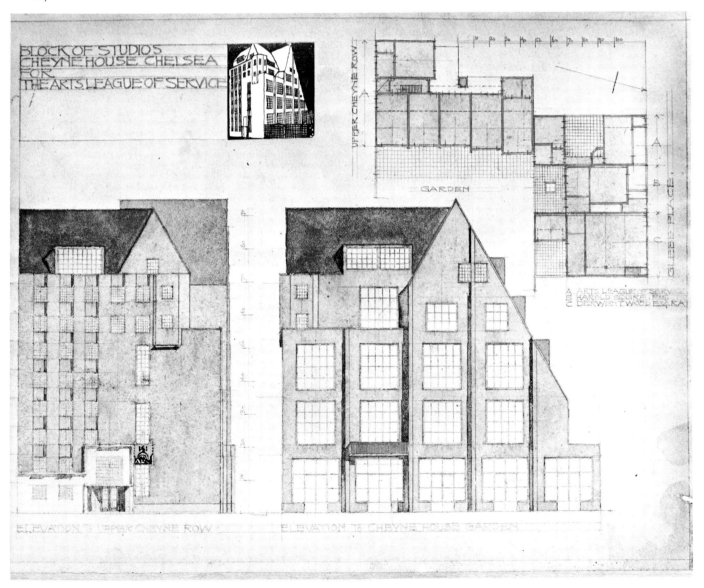

1920

Proposed theatre in Chelsea for Margaret Morris, a dancer and teacher of dancing. This was Mackintosh's last architectural work. Objections from the Ecclesiastical Commissioners, on whose land the theatre was to be built, were eventually overcome, but again insufficient funds led to the project being abandoned.
Drawings are in the University of Glasgow Mackintosh Collection.

Right — Design for a proposed theatre in Chelsea, front elevation and cross sections, 1920. Pen and ink, pencil and wash 44 × 72 cm. (UGMC)

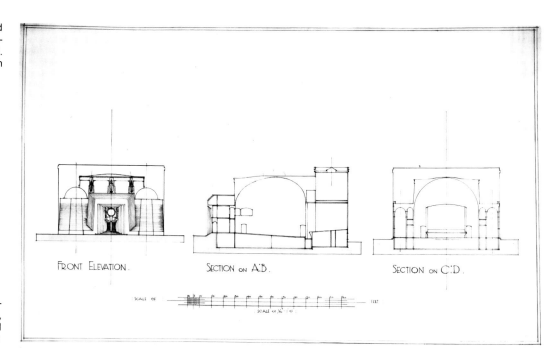

FRONT ELEVATION.   SECTION ON A.B.   SECTION ON C.D.

Below — Design for a proposed theatre in Chelsea, plans, 1920. Pen and ink, pencil and wash, 44.6 × 72.1 cm. (UGMC)

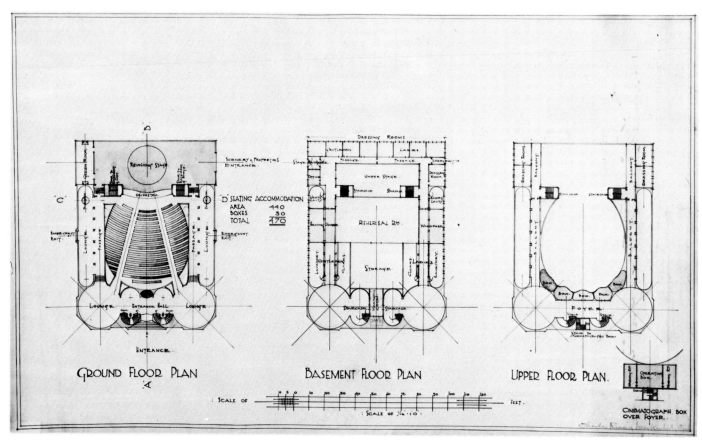

GROUND FLOOR PLAN   BASEMENT FLOOR PLAN   UPPER FLOOR PLAN.

106

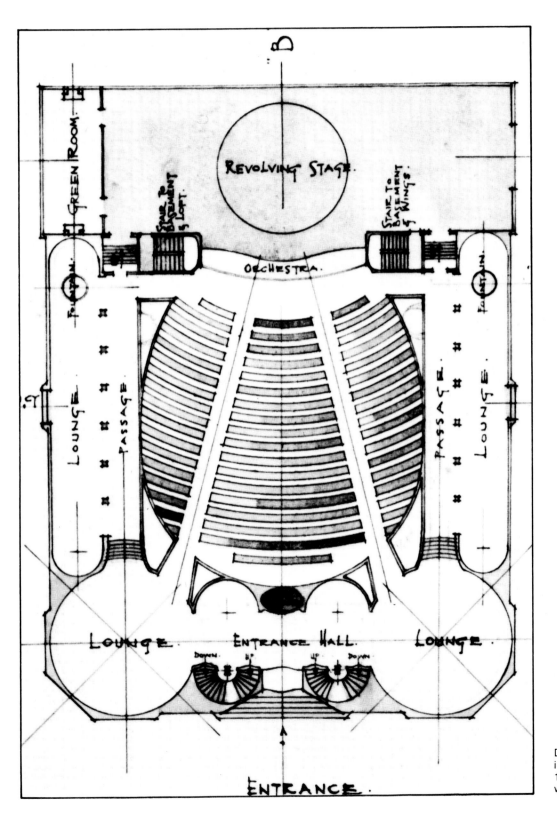

REVOLVING STAGE.

STAIR TO BASEMENT & LOFT.

STAIR TO BASEMENT & WINGS.

GREEN ROOM.

ORCHESTRA.

LOUNGE.

PASSAGE.

PASSAGE.

LOUNGE.

LOUNGE.

ENTRANCE HALL.

LOUNGE.

DOWN   UP   UP   DOWN

ENTRANCE.

Design for a proposed theatre in Chelsea, ground floor plan, 1920. Pen and ink, pencil and wash. (UGMC)

MACKINTOSH COLLECTIONS IN SCOTLAND

Hunterian Art Gallery, University of Glasgow, Mackintosh Collection
The major body of Mackintosh's work is owned by the University of Glasgow, the residuary legatees of Mackintosh's Estate. The collection comprises over 600 drawings and designs including architectural drawings, plans and elevations, watercolours, designs for furniture, interiors, textiles, and graphics, and over 60 pieces of furniture. The majority of the furniture is on permanent display in The Mackintosh Wing of the Hunterian Art Gallery which contains the reconstructed principal interiors from the architect's Glasgow home at 78 Southpark Avenue.

The Glasgow School of Art
The Glasgow School of Art possesses watercolours by Charles Rennie Mackintosh and Margaret MacDonald Mackintosh, a fine collection of Mackintosh's original drawings for the School of Art and an extensive collection of furniture, much of it in daily use. The School also has several Mackintosh light fittings and a very fine selection of wrought ironwork, most of which is an integral part of the structure. Since the School is primarily an educational establishment, visitors are reminded that, while they may be shown some of the more interesting parts of the building if a janitor is available to guide them, the collections themselves are only available for inspection by previous appointment.

Art Gallery and Museum, Kelvingrove, Glasgow
The Department of Fine Art has a small though important group of Mackintosh watercolours. The Department of Decorative Art possesses the major part of the interior fittings and furniture from the Ingram Street Tearooms, as well as other items of Mackintosh furniture and a major collection of work by Mackintosh's contemporaries.

The Charles Rennie Mackintosh Society
The Charles Rennie Mackintosh Society was founded in 1973 to foster interest in the work of Mackintosh in the belief that an informed and enthusiastic public is the surest protection against any neglect and destruction of the architect's remaining work. In 1977 the Society procured the lease of Queen's Cross Church which it has undertaken to restore and maintain, and which is now in use as the Society headquarters.

The Society is registered as a charity and has been encouraged by many generous grants. Its committee offers specialist advice to owners and interested parties on the restoration and maintenance of Mackintosh buildings. The Society also publishes a quarterly newsletter and sells postcards, posters, books and notecards printed with Mackintosh designs.

SELECTED BIBLIOGRAPHY

Books
Alison, Filippo, *Charles Rennie Mackintosh as a Designer of Chairs*, Milan and New York, 1973, London, 1978.
Billcliffe, Roger, *Architectural Sketches and Flower Drawings by Charles Rennie Mackintosh*, London, 1977.
Billcliffe, Roger, *Charles Rennie Mackintosh — The Complete Furniture, Furniture Drawings and Interior Designs*, Guildford and London, 1978.
Billcliffe, Roger, *Mackintosh Watercolours*, London, 1978.
Doak, Archibald M. (ed.), *Architectural Jottings by Charles Rennie Mackintosh*, selected by Andrew McLaren Young, Glasgow Institute of Architects, 1968.
Howarth, Thomas, *Charles Rennie Mackintosh and the Modern Movement*, London, 1952, second edition 1977.
Larner, Gerald and Celia, *The Glasgow Style*, Edinburgh, 1979.
Macleod, Robert, *Charles Rennie Mackintosh*, London 1968.
Pevsner, Nikolaus, *Pioneers of Modern Design*, (revised ed.), Harmondsworth & Baltimore, 1968.
Pevsner, Nikolaus, *Sources of Modern Architecture and Design*, London, 1968.
Rowland, Kurt, *A History of the Modern Movement: Art, Architecture and Design*, New York and London, 1973.
Walker, David and Gomme, Andor, *Architecture of Glasgow*, London, 1968.
Wittkower, R. (ed.), *Studies in Western Art: Problems of the Nineteenth and Twentieth Centuries*, Princeton, 1963.

Articles
Beazley, Elisabeth and Lambert, Sam, 'The Astonishing City, Glasgow', *Architect's Journal*, vol. 139, 6 May, 1964, pp. 1006-1036.
Brimey, Marcus, 'The Glitter of Mackintosh', *The Architectural Review*, vol. 144, Dec. 1968, p.345. Objects in silver designed by Mackintosh.
Brimey, Marcus, 'An Architect of Unfulfilled Promise', *Country Life*, vol. 144, 7 Nov. 1968, pp. 1182-83.
Chapman-Huston, Desmond, 'Charles Rennie Mackintosh, His Life and Work', *Artwork*, vol. 7, no. 21, Spring 1930.
Futagawa, Yukio (ed.), 'Charles Rennie Mackintosh — The Glasgow School of Art', *Global Architecture* 49, Tokyo, 1979. Text by Andy MacMillan.
Godwin, W., 'House for an Art Lover', *American Architect and Building News*, vol. 85, 24 Sept. 1904, p. 105, pl. 150.
Godwin, W., 'Rennie Mackintosh, Victor Horta and Berlage', *Journal of the Architectural Association*, vol. 65, Feb. 1950, pp. 140-5.
Howarth, Thomas, 'Charles Rennie Mackintosh (1867-1933)', *Country Life*, 1939.
Howarth, Thomas, 'Some Mackintosh Furniture Preserved', *The Architectural Review*, vol. 100, Aug. 1946, pp. 33-4.
Howarth, Thomas, 'Mackintosh and the Scottish Tradition', *Magazine of Art*, vol. 41, Nov. 1948, pp. 264-7.
Howarth, Thomas, 'Charles Rennie Mackintosh (1868-1928): Architect and Designer', *Journal of the R.I.B.A.*, vol. 58, Nov. 1950, pp. 15-19.
Pevsner, Nikolaus, 'C.R.Mackintosh', 1950. Monograph in the *Architetti del Movimento Moderno* series, Il Balcone, Milan.
Pevsner, Nikolaus, 'No Grace for Mackintosh', *Architectural Review*, vol. 118, Aug. 1955, pp. 117-8.
Rubino, Luciano, 'La Mano di Mackintosh', *L'architettura*, vol. 13, May and July, 1967, pp. 60-4; 200-4; 270-4.

Rykwert, Joseph, 'Charles Rennie Mackintosh, 1868-1928', *Domus*, no. 462, 1968, pp. 32.

Shand, Philip Morton, 'Scenario for a Human Drama: The Glasgow Interlude', *The Architectural Review,* vol. 77, Jan. 1935, pp. 23-6.

Shand, Philip Morton, 'C.R. Mackintosh', *Journal of the Architectural Association,* vol. 75, Jan. 1959, pp. 163-7.

Sturrock, Mary, 'Remembering Charles Rennie Mackintosh', *The Connoisseur*, vol. 183, no. 738, Aug. 1973, pp. 280-8. A recorded interview.

Summerson, John, 'Studies in Western Art: Some British Contemporaries of Frank Lloyd Wright'. Paper delivered to International Congress of the History of Art.

Taylor, E.A., 'Charles Rennie Mackintosh — a Neglected Genius', *The Studio*, vol. 105, 1933, pp. 344-52.

Walker, David, 'Charles Rennie Mackintosh', *The Architectural Review*, vol. 144, Nov. 1968, pp. 355 et seq.

Zevi, Bruno, 'Charles Rennie Mackintosh, Poeta di uno Strumento Perduto: La Linea', *Mentron,* no. 40, 1951, pp. 24-35.

Catalogues

Barnes, H. Jefferson, *Charles Rennie Mackintosh: Furniture,* Glasgow School of Art, 1964. Selected examples from the School of Art Collection.

Barnes, H. Jefferson, *Charles Rennie Mackintosh: Ironwork and Metalwork,* Glasgow School of Art, 1964. Selected examples from the School of Art Collection.

Billcliffe, Roger, *Flower drawings by Charles Rennie Mackintosh,* University of Glasgow 1977. Catalogue of the exhibition at the Hunterian Museum.

Billcliffe, Roger, *Mackintosh Watercolours,* Glasgow Art Gallery in association with The Fine Art Society, 1978. Catalogue of Mackintosh's watercolours exhibition, Glasgow and London, 1978.

Bliss, Douglas Percy, *Charles Rennie Mackintosh and the Glasgow School of Art,* Glasgow School of Art, 1961.

Glasgow School of Art Prospectus, 1968-1969, with an introduction on the Mackintosh Centenary.

Howarth, Thomas, *Charles Rennie Mackintosh (1868-1928),* Saltine Soceity, Edinburgh, 1953. Catalogue for the 1953 Edinburgh Festival Exhibition of Mackintosh's work.

MacLaren Young, Andrew, *Charles Rennie Mackintosh 1868-1928: Architecture, Design and Painting,* Edinburgh Festival Society, 1968. Catalogue for the 1968 Mackintosh exhibition arranged by the Scottish Arts Council and Edinburgh Festival Society.

Sekler, Edward, 'Mackintosh und Wien', in *Charles Rennie Mackintosh,* Museum of the Twentieth Century, Vienna, 1969. Catalogue for the 1969 Mackintosh Exhibition in Vienna, sponsored by the British Council. Introduction by Andrew MacLaren Young.

ADDENDA

Books

Dixon, Elizabeth (ed.), *Charles Rennie Mackintosh: A Selective Bibliography,* Architectural Association, London, 1981

Russell, Frank (ed.), *Art Nouveau Architecture,* London, 1979.

Article

Billcliffe, Roger, 'Hill House 1902-04, *Architectural Design: New Free Style,* vol. 50 1/2- 1980, pp 72-5.

Catalogue

Some Designs by C R Mackintosh, The Architectural Association, London, 1981.

INDEX

KEY TO MACKINTOSH BUILDINGS

1 **Glasgow Herald Building**, corner of Mitchell Street and Mitchell Lane.

2 **Martyr's Public School**, Parson Street.

3 **Glasgow School of Art**, 167 Renfrew Street.

4 **Queen's Cross Church**, 866 Garscube Road.

5 **Ruchill Church Hall**, 24 Ruchill Street. About ½ mile beyond Queen's Cross, off Maryhill.

*6 **Windyhill**, Kilmacolm. Bus from Waterloo Street and train from Central Station. Glasgow 17 miles.

7 **Daily Record Building**, Renfield Lane.

8 **Hill House**, Helensburg. Train from Queen Street Station. Glasgow 23 miles. Property of the Royal Incorporation of Architects in Scotland — Hill House Trust. Tel. Helensburg 3900 for details of opening times.

9 **Willow Tea Room**, 199 Sauchiehall Street. Now part of Daly's Store.

10 **Scotland Street School**, Scotland Street. Near Shields Road underground station.

11 **Redclyffe**, 140 Balgrayhill Road.

*12 **Mosside**, Kilmacolm. Bus from Waterloo Street and train from Central Station. Glasgow 17 miles.

13 **Auchenibert**, Killearn. Bus from Buchanan Street Bus Station. Glasgow 16 miles.

* These are private houses which can only be visited with the permission of the owner.

For public collections see page 108